ski touring

the Regnery Guide to ski touring

sven Wiik and David sumner

Henry Regnery Company · Chicago

Library of Congress Cataloging in Publication Data

Wiik, Sven.
  Ski touring.

  Includes bibliographical references.
  1. Cross-country skiing. I. Sumner, David, joint
author. II. Title.
GV854.9.C7W54   796.9'3   74-6921
ISBN 0-8092-8367-0
ISBN 0-8092-8366-2 (pbk.)

To Paul W. Wright
former Director of Athletics,
Western State College, Gunnison, Colorado
—with thanks for many years of educational
opportunities, experiences, and support

To Omar Stephen Swenson, 1879–1966
—for all those years of unfailing warmth
and wisdom

Published by Henry Regnery Company
180 North Michigan Avenue, Chicago, Illinois 60601
Manufactured in the United States of America
Library of Congress Catalog Card Number: 74-6921
International Standard Book Number: 0-8092-8367-0 (cloth)
                                    0-8092-8366-2 (paper)

Contents

Acknowledgments

No book falls together without the help of at least a few good souls who volunteer their time, thoughts, and criticism to the beleaguered authors. Fortunately, the touring fraternity is especially rich in such willingness. Those we would especially like to thank are Bob Tucker of Gerry/Nordic; Bob Bruce and Bob McFetridge of Holubar Mountaineering; Charlie Meyers of the Denver Post; Wayne Merry of Yosemite Mountaineering; Olof von Fieleitzen at the Kungliga Biblioteket in Stockholm; Joe Pete Wilson of North American Nordic; Ernest Wilkinson, veteran trapper, digger of profound snow caves, and wise follower of animal tracks; Birgitta Wiik; the infamous brothers Quinn, Don and Dave; Al McClelland of Rocky Mountain Expeditions; and Judy Sumner, who endured lengthy oral readings of this manuscript as it labored into being.

Photo Credits

Dick Armstrong, Institute of Alpine and Arctic Research, page 138
Denver Public Library, Western History Department, page xiv
Virginia Huidekoper, pages 99 (top), 166 (top)
Alexis Kelner, pages xxi, 6, 96, 126, 141, 146
Fletcher Manley, pages 2, 130
Charlie Meyers, page 172
Bettina Mueller, pages xiv, 99 (bottom)
North American Nordic, pages xv, xvii
Norwegian Information Service, page xi
Buzz Soard, pages 3, 116
David Sumner, pages x, xix, 5, 8-36, 46-93, 100-113, 132, 135, 150-155, 166 (bottom), 167 (bottom left)
Judy Sumner, pages 38, 167 (top and bottom right)
Eric Varney and Holubar Mountaineering, pages viii,165
Ernest Wilkinson, pages 123, 170
Peter Wingle, pages 128, 144
Yosemite Mountaineering, pages 98, 175

Introduction: Good Morning, Ski Touring

The first positive thing that can be said for ski touring is that, in one way or another, man has been doing it for literally thousands of years. Over those long centuries, the purpose of skiing has changed from survival to pleasure, but the basic ski has stayed the same. Like the wheel, the ski has hung on doggedly, accepted infinite improvements and embellishments, and come out looking pretty much the same. The activity has also been unchanged; the late Stone Age nomad whose 4,500-year-old ski was dug from a marshy bog not far below the Arctic Circle, near the Swedish village of Hoting, probably strode along more or less as does a skier in the 1970s. Man's manner of walking hasn't changed significantly in the last forty-five centuries; it follows that his basic style of ski touring hasn't either.

Knowing that the roots of this sport go so far back into the past won't help you glide up a hill any more easily today, but there's something reassuring in knowing about those ancient beginnings. We live in an age that is in love with whatever is

Sven Wiik ready to ski.

new. And, while modern touring is a recent arrival on the American scene, it has come largely as a revival, not as one more gesture in our nervous national quest for novelty. Unlike such fleeting crazes as pop art, canasta, the hula hoop, and, yes, even streaking, touring has a long history, a firm foundation. It's a basic, time-tested activity, and there's little reason to doubt it has returned to stay.

But what about those Stone Age skis at Hoting, the very oldest yet discovered? Though earlier skis may have been made of bone, these were of pine. They were wide and stubby—less than 4½ feet (110 cm) long and just over 4 inches (10.4 cm) wide, with slightly raised footstands, square tails, and upturned tips. The bindings, which were probably leather and threaded through a notch in the ski, were single toestraps. The skis' overall construction gives the clear impression that, even though he worked with a primitive stone tool, the person who made these knew what he was doing. In other words, he was hardly the first human to fashion himself a pair of skis; their true origin lies beyond our reach—buried deep in the hidden recesses of the past.

And how did this early Swedish craftsman use the skis? Very naturally, for getting around in the winter; more specifically, for hunting. Some miles to the west of Hoting, on the Norwegian island of Rødøy, there is a remarkable stone carving, or petroglyph, which dates back about 4,000 years. Elk, reindeer, seals, and porpoise are carved at random on the rock, and near the center is a lone figure on skis, which are much longer than those unearthed at Hoting. This man is obviously a hunter; instead of anything resembling modern poles, he carries what appears to be an axe. For some strange reason, his ears are long, like those of an elk, perhaps to signify some identity with his quarry. Why was this carving done? It's hard to say. Perhaps it is a record or celebration of triumphs; more likely it is a kind of magical invocation designed to give the hunter power over the elusive animals he tracked.

Ski touring in the Stone Age—a petroglyph on the Norwegian island of Rødøy.

Those skis unquestionably gave Stone Age man tremendous advantages in the winter; in some cases, hunting on skis was too effective, causing a scarcity of game. Norway's 1274 Code of Laws forbade men on skis to pursue elk, as it was too easy "to catch up with the animals in the deep snow and kill them."

More graphic is the account from the thirteenth-century Norwegian book, *The King's Mirror*. "As soon as a man binds long pieces of wood to the feet," it reads, "he conquers the birds in their flight, the swiftest running dogs, and the reindeer that run twice as fast as the deer. There are many hunters who can use their skis so well that they can hit nine reindeer with their spears." Those same spears were also used to fend off bears and wolves and, perhaps more significantly, as "braking poles" that could be dragged forcefully in the snow to slow a downhill descent or serve as a rudder in making a turn.

A person could easily become absorbed in studying the rich and varied history of skiing. One could note the distinct kinds of skis that appeared independently and more or less simultaneously down through the Bronze and Iron Ages, all the way from Siberia across the Ural Mountains west to Norway— long skis and short, skis with fur-clad bottoms (usually seal or reindeer skin) for better traction going up hills, others with upturned tails as well as tips so they could be reversed in case one broke, still others that were maneuvered with steering ropes tied to the tips. Another area of study is the wild and bloody Norse myths and sagas, with their heroic accounts of Ullr and Skade, legendary gods of skiing and the hunt. A student could trace all kinds of records from the Middle Ages on, in which skiing and the exploits of skiers play a central role. He could note the emergence of the ski as a weapon of war (Norway's first ski troops were organized in 1716) and how this military use led first to formal drills and then to competitions.

The ski came across the Atlantic to the United States with Scandinavian immigrants who settled first in the upper midwest (this region, not New England, is properly the cradle of

American skiing) and later pressed on to the mountain mine camps of the Rockies and the Sierras, where the ski was commonly known as the "Norwegian snowshoe." About 1840, a young Norwegian farm boy, Sondre Nordheim, invented the "osier binding"—thin woven shoots of birch roots that wrapped *around the heel* and for the first time in over 4,000 years anchored the foot firmly to the ski. Nordheim revolutionized skiing; suddenly skis could be turned and maneuvered like ice skates. Competitions followed naturally—the first open cross-country race was held in 1843, the first jumping event in 1866.

THE NORWEGIAN SNOWSHOE

It wasn't a snowshoe at all, but rather a ski, 9 to 14 feet long, stiff and handhewn from a single cutting of Engelmann spruce. Around the early Colorado mine camps of the 1880s—Crested Butte, Gothic, and even today's alpine mecca at Aspen—the Norwegian snowshoe was a wintertime necessity. Either one holed up in his cabin or he skied for supplies, for companionship, or just to ease wintertime bouts of cabin fever. The Colorado old-timers actually preferred their skis long rather than short, for these rode more easily over bumps and depressions in the snow.

The tips of these giant snowshoes curled upward from 4 to 6 inches. The curling was accomplished by steaming one end of a nearly finished ski and then bending it around a large log (18 inches in diameter was about right) to the proper curvature. Bindings were thick leather straps. Behind the bindings a narrow strip of wood was screwed into the footstand to block in the heel and keep it from slipping backward.

The pole was something else. A single tough sapling from 7 to 9 feet long did the job and was used at one side for support, as a brake, and as a kind of auxiliary rudder to help when making turns. If this pole broke, a replacement could soon be chopped from a nearby tree.

The old sourdoughs even used wax! It was beeswax—sometimes applied with a hot iron, sometimes simply rubbed on cold. It was pretty slow when one started out but seemed to improve with wear as the skier glided along.

The name "Norwegian snowshoe" was commonplace back in the 80s; those webbed contraptions one normally associates with the term were known as "Canadian snowshoes," to eliminate any confusion.

Downhill running on the
"Norwegian snowshoe,"
1887.

The long, rich history of ski touring, however, is not the only positive thing that can be said of the sport. Without slighting downhill skiers, whose numbers also continue to grow across the United States, one can assert with good reason that touring is the foundation of all skiing—the beginning and the end of the sport for those who participate.

For the beginner touring is one of the most sensible ways to learn the basics of skiing, safely and gradually. When you start out on the flat, there is little or none of the fear that so often occurs upon one's initial introduction to alpine skiing. In fact, it is a tremendous leap for a non-skier to begin downhill work right away. Not only must the beginner develop the necessary balance and coordination; he must also cope with the slope, the inevitable falls, the challenge of speed, and the burden of heavy equipment (especially the boots), which many newcomers often find cumbersome and unmanageable.

But even a child as young as two or three can start out on a pair of children's touring skis. He can flop around on the flat and learn the basics of coordination and balance at his own pace as his body grows; he can also gain a comfortable, relaxed familiarity with the world of winter. You can no more put a three-year-old on a pair of downhill skis than you can put him behind the wheel of a car. Touring skis (with simple leather bindings that fit an everyday overshoe) are easier to adjust to and can become a part of the child's early learning experiences.

When a toddler explores his yard, local park or nearby meadow, he inevitably encounters hills and bumps and develops ways of first coping with them, then enjoying them. The Scandinavians take advantage of this curiosity; while most American children play with a tricycle or sled by age two or three, Norwegian, Swedish and Finnish children test themselves on skis.

Later, as the Scandinavian child grows, he often begins to specialize, to develop particular skills. By age eight to twelve, some have moved to downhill skiing, to jumping or to junior cross-country racing. Others continue to putter happily along as recreational tour skiers. One thing is common to all: with comparatively little fear or frustration, Scandinavian children are at home on skis. The necessary balance and coordination have come naturally, over time. The taste for winter has done likewise.

For the adult, this pattern is well worth noting. Some experts in the touring community have even suggested that all first-time skiers start out with a season or two of touring before attempting to tackle the slopes. Although the idea might seem heretical to many, it could eliminate the fears and frustrations common to the first ski experience, and, in the end, create a generation of more confident, relaxed, and able skiers.

If touring is the foundation for all skiing, its benefits accrue not only to the beginner but also to the older skier who has become wary of risking more brittle limbs on the downhill slopes. Many skiers, after years at the alpine sport, hang up their downhill skis and return to the sport as they began it, on the touring trail. "Langlaufer Leben Langer" ("Tour skiers live longer") is a favorite Swiss motto these days. Of the old timers in this sport, none is more legendary than the Canadian, Herman "Jack Rabbit" Johannsen, now in his ripe, sprightly nineties and still touring up to six hours daily. Though not even touring's greatest advocates would maintain that no bones have been broken along the 4,500-year-old touring trail, the number has been few and far between.

As the foundation for all skiing, touring is also an excellent early-season conditioner for the alpine buff. Come those first big snows of November or December, the temptation to beat a rapid track to the nearest mountain can be overwhelming; the potential hazard of overdoing it, due to summer-slackened muscles, is quite high. Two or three days of touring, even of the modest variety, will ease those aching muscles, and the risks associated with them. Touring will bring muscles back into tone and balance back into tune. Or, put it this way: the best way to get into condition for skiing is to ski.

Although there are several advantages of touring, none adequately explain the sudden surge of the sport across the North American snowbelt. Only a decade ago, touring was restricted almost exclusively to cross-country racing and a few scattered circles of maverick ski mountaineers. Today the boom is well-established and shows no sign of abating.

Statistics describing the growth of touring in the United States are difficult to obtain, although general evidence is ample. Backpacking shops that specialize in touring equipment during the winter are increasing and flourishing. Lodges that offer certified instruction and various group tours are doing well, also. One after another, major alpine areas have added substantial touring programs. Many national forests are under tremendous pressure to plan and establish more touring trails. The major national parks (Yosemite, Yellowstone, Glacier, and Mount Rainier, for example) today count on a substantial winter influx of tour skiers and snow campers. Citizens' touring races, which didn't even exist five years ago, are now attracting thousands of entrants. This healthy list goes on. If one still insists on more specific statistics regarding the growth of the sport, the closest he will come is the number of skis annually imported into the United States from Scandinavia (and increasingly, from central Europe). This number has been absolutely ballooning. Back in 1967 a mere 7,000 pairs of touring skis crossed the Atlantic to the American market; by 1970, the figure had increased to 40,000, and by 1973 to a whopping 340,000. If that doesn't say it, nothing will.

During this period, it's become fashionable to say that the ski touring boom represents a disenchantment with alpine skiing—especially its crowded slopes, high prices, and sometimes overbearing commercialism. This is unlikely. Alpine skiing's negative aspects cannot begin to account for the surge of genuine, heartfelt enthusiasm that surrounds touring in the United States today. Negative reasons are seldom the basis for anything in which this much pleasure is involved. Of the obvious and positive reasons for touring's recent surge in popularity, the following seem to stand out.

Touring and the Outdoors. Currently, the largest number of people taking up touring are also those who head for the hills in the spring, summer, and fall: backpackers, hikers, walkers, fishermen, campers, hunters, and nature photographers. For them, touring has converted the "off-season" into a fresh, inviting opportunity; winter has become a season of discovery rather than one of sitting inside and waiting for spring.

Touring as a Skill. Arbitrarily, one might say that about 10 percent of the joy of downhill skiing is in the alpine scenery; while the other 90 percent derives from mastering technique—the pleasure of carving graceful turns, making high speed descents, and so forth. Just the opposite balance could apply to backpacking; 90 percent of its satisfaction comes from the scenery, 10 percent from technique—efficient walking, sensible pacing and the like.

Touring provides the best of both worlds in a happy, 50-50 combination. It offers both the delight in the outdoors and the pleasure of perfecting a skill and enjoying the freedom mastery gives. When a backpacker tops a hill, he has no choice but to trudge down the other side; the tour skier has all kinds of options. Even when simply gliding along the flat, the tour skier always has technique to occupy his mind; he can work on it, play with it, or just observe it.

Touring and the Family. Touring is a relaxed, basically safe sport; something one generation can readily enjoy with the next. This does happen, and often. Touring is intrinsically a group activity—something people do and enjoy together.

Touring and Fitness. As does no other recreational activity except swimming, touring exercises the whole body. Arms, legs, lungs, and heart all work rhythmically together when you're out there gliding along. You don't have to be particularly fit to take up this sport, but the more you tour, the more your fitness is bound to improve.

Touring and Ease. Beginning tour skiers are often dumbfounded at the long distances they cover, even on their very first ventures on the trail. They're equally amazed when they don't collapse in aching heaps at the end of the day.

There are at least three good reasons for this. First, unlike the hiker and backpacker, the tour skier does not have to lift his feet; instead he simply slides them along, expending 50 percent less energy. Also, the tour skier gets a free ride down all hills and slopes (courtesy of gravity, wax, and snow). Finally, with each stride on his skis, even the beginner will find himself gliding along for an extra six inches or more—a bonus absolutely unavailable to the hiker. Remember: the ski is essentially a means of transportation. It's a specialized extension of your leg that enables you to travel farther, faster, and with more efficiency. Of course it should be an improvement over mere walking.

Finally, a word about this book. For the most part it is written for the beginner, the person who never before has

ventured forth on touring skis. We've tried to pack it with usable, common-sense information that will not only get you going but also serve as a handy reference guide as you progress. As much as possible, chapters have been organized around distinct elements of the touring sport; but here and there where it has seemed wise to avoid unnecessary page flipping, we've allowed some overlap. Many of the details we've covered you'll read once, assimilate, and never consciously think of again. Others you may wish to return to several times or more.

One special note: as you proceed through the latter pages of this book, you'll notice much attention is given to safety and survival—to such potential dangers as avalanches, frostbite, exposure, and snow-blindness. This could create the wrong impression, but do not be scared off; none of these hazards are in any way intrinsic to touring—*if* you're careful and *if* you exercise sensible foresight. As we will repeat several times in this book, winter conditions do reduce one's margin of error. Our concern in pointing out where mistakes can lead is purely cautionary. Most people tour for years and never return home with anything worse than a mild sunburn. May you be one of those.

There's an old adage, sadly not followed as often as it should be, that goes like this: "The purpose of a good teacher is to make himself utterly useless." When all is said and done, we'd like to think of this book as such a teacher. Take from it what you need to make touring the pleasure you desire. When you've reached that point, discard The Regnery Guide to Ski Touring or, better yet, give it to a friend. It's done all it can do for you.

From then on the snow, the frost, the sun, the wide open spaces, the woods, and the brisk winter winds will be your teachers. You can learn much more from them, anyway.

I
Where Do You Start?

So you've decided to try ski touring. Where do you start?

Before you purchase the equipment, you're going to have to make a very simple, basic decision. You will have to decide what kind of touring to try. Since you're brand new to the sport, that could well sound impossible. Don't worry. It isn't. In all likelihood you already know more than you think: more than enough to start out where you want.

There are four clearly defined groups of ski tourers. You cannot avoid falling into one of these; there is simply nowhere else to fall. The choice is yours.

THE RACER

Cross-country racing has been around for a long time. Many people first become aware of the entire sport's existence through this very specialized and demanding version of it. They've seen racing in the Olympics on TV; or, if they live in

1

Cross-country racers at the Sapporo Olympics, 1972.

certain parts of the snowbelt, they know there are some students on the local college (or sometimes even high school) ski teams who go in for cross-country racing. Even so, the racers are at most 3 percent of today's growing legion of ski tourers.

The racer usually runs on a carefully groomed trail or track. He is in peak condition and skis hard and for long distances. Competition is intense, both against other racers and against his own physical limits. This dimension of the sport is also the most exacting; skiing technique must be refined until the skier is like a smoothly functioning machine; waxing is both intricate and arcane; equipment is specialized, carefully engineered, and ultralight.

THE LIGHT TOUR SKIER

About 90 percent of all people touring today in the United States fall into this category. The odds are almost overwhelming that this is where you, too, will probably start out. Since the

Light tour skiing at Ashcroft, near Aspen, Colorado.

demands are slight, and the equipment light and easily handled, it's a natural enough place to begin.

The light tour skier does most of his skiing on an already broken trail. With more and more alpine ski areas, national parks, national forests, communities, and clubs maintaining trails of all lengths and degrees of difficulty, good routes are not hard to find. The better trails are laid out over varied terrain, and through interesting country. Some may be less than a mile—a simple run through a pleasant wood or over the last three holes of a rolling golf course. Others are longer, but no less interesting, and no less fun.

The light tour skier need not be in any special physical condition. If you can walk around the block, mow the lawn, or manage a morning's stroll in a city park, you can also handle light ski touring. Many people start in just this shape (or non-shape); invariably they discover that even this least demanding type of touring soon begins to improve their overall physical fitness.

Once started, the light tour skier will also want to work on improving his technique, primarily because it makes the sport easier, more relaxing, and more enjoyable. Improved technique leads to greater speed—which in itself can often be fun (contrary to what many people believe, superior conditioning does not mean speed in touring; it merely gives the skier the endurance needed to stay in high gear over long distances).

Occasionally the light tour skier will want to venture into the unbroken snow and do some casual exploring and poking about the woods. He may lead his family on a winter picnic, perhaps to check out a favorite summer hiking area they've never seen under snow. After a time, the skier might also want to take a crack at one of the many citizens' races that are springing up around the country. The point of these events is not to exhaust oneself, but rather to make it from start to finish at a respectable, enjoyable pace. Entrants have been known to pause en route for a rest, and to partake of some communal cheese and wine.

THE TOUR SKIER

Now we're back to the minority—to that independent soul who heads straight out into the unbroken snow. The destination might be a favorite ice-fishing hole, a summer cabin 5 miles from the end of the plowed road, a wilderness area, or one of thousands of other out-of-the-way spots. Racing holds no interest for this skier; predetermined trails are usually against his principles.

The tour skier will have to be in respectable condition. Often he is a summertime backpacker, and wants to extend this love to a year-round activity. As it is for the light tour skier, technique is important to him as a means of making the sport more relaxing, less tiring, and more pleasurable.

Tour skiers now comprise about 5 percent of all people involved in the sport, though their numbers are gaining steadily. In many parts of the United States, professional guides and

Tour skiing under full packs in the Colorado Rockies.

outfitters have discovered tour skiing and lead groups on moderate winter journeys. The Sierra Club, for example, lists tour skiing trips as part of its extensive outings program, and has recently published a nifty little hip pocket "totebook" entitled *Wilderness Skiing* (for both the tour skier and the ski mountaineer).

THE SKI MOUNTAINEER

At the far end of the spectrum is another skier who, like the racer, seeks extreme challenges. Mountaineering demands top conditioning. A confirmed trailbreaker, an explorer, a searcher after summits, a person who delights in the long downhill run from the top, the ski mountaineer still relies on touring equipment (though it will be tougher and heavier), on touring technique (though he will spice in alpine maneuvers on his descents), and on using waxes (though he may turn to old-fashioned sealskins for steep climbs).

Ski mountaineers in the Lone Peak Wilderness, northern Utah.

Very few people start as ski mountaineers. Prior skill in downhill skiing, in heavy summertime climbing, and in backpacking are advised prerequisites. The ski mountaineer must be accustomed to long safaris and to toting a heavy load.

(To avoid confusion of terms at this point, one final group needs mention—albeit only in parentheses. This is the *alpine tour skier*; truthfully, he dwells on the barest fringe of the touring sport. His equipment, more often than not, is of the standard alpine variety, with modified bindings to allow at least a nominal heel lift and stride. He does rely on touring technique, hampered as it may be by the cumbersome gear, for one admirable purpose only. He *walks and climbs* to dizzying, remote mountain heights—far from the lifts and the crowds —in order to enjoy incredibly long, dazzling, deep powder downhill descents to the valleys below. At present, those mysteriously named ranges of the Canadian Rockies—the Bugaboos, the Cariboos, and the Monashees—are the heartland of alpine ski touring in North America.)

Those are the choices open to anyone interested in ski touring. The range is vast, the experiences varied. Drop in where you will.

2

Equipment

What kind of equipment are you going to buy? It depends on the touring category you wish to join; each requires different gear for the enjoyment of different dimensions of the sport.

There is, however, one cardinal rule for whatever choice you make: go *as light as you can without sacrificing strength, support, and stability.* If you really want to race, then your equipment can be ultralight. If you want to tackle challenges such as the John Muir Trail in the Sierras or the more weather-beaten reaches of the White Mountains in New Hampshire, your equipment had better be durable and tough, which means it will be heavier, too.

Never carry any more weight than you have to. It's just more work, and that's not what touring is about.

RACING EQUIPMENT

Even though you probably won't buy any, it's wise for the recreational skier to keep an eye cocked toward what's happening with racing equipment. As in downhill skiing, this is where the breakthroughs in high-performance technology and design first show up; a look at where racing gear is today will usually forecast the direction in which recreational equipment is heading in the next year or two.

First rule for racing equipment: skis, poles, boots, and bindings should all be extremely light. There is no need for anything but the absolute minimum.

Skis

The racing ski is narrow, less than 2 inches across under the boot (about 46 to 49 millimeters). It is very light, seldom more than 3 pounds. It should also have excellent flexibility, body, and spring, so that it can follow the ups and downs of the track like a snake at high speed.

Prior to February 17, 1974, it might have been natural to assume that racing skis (and all other touring skis as well) would be made of laminated wood. After all, wood had been the established material for centuries. While Scandinavian manufacturers had carefully refined wood ski technology to an art, generations of enthusiasts had become fondly attached to the handsome rubbed, lacquered, or varnished results for both functional and aesthetic reasons. Wood was to the touring ski as pigskin is to the football; the relationship was assumed to be immutable.

Or so it seemed until that historic February day at Falun, Sweden, when in the men's World Championship 30-kilometer race, a wave of synthetic fiber glass skis appeared to dominate the field and win the event. Then, as if to prove this unexpected onslaught was no fluke, the tide turned even more heavily in favor of fiber glass in the ensuing men's 50-kilometer race. By the time the championships were concluded, Kneissel's computer-designed glass skis had taken a grand total of twelve medals; Fischer's similar model was close behind. Scandinavia's wood ski makers were openly shocked and talked catastrophe, while the touring world as a whole was on notice that a revolution in ski technology had arrived.

Today, the transition from wood to glass is still in progress, with the result that the entire touring ski market is more varied than ever before in its history. Reduced to their essentials, you'll find three different kinds of skis on today's market.

All wood skis. Like other wood touring skis, racing models are made of multiple laminations (16 to 32 is standard) of birch, hickory, beech, ash, and spruce. Lamination is obviously important; the proper mix of wood types gives a ski the appropriate blend of flexibility and strength and helps prevent warping. In racing skis especially, some of the interior laminations are balsa, or else long, hollow air channels; this makes the ski that much lighter. Cross-country runners have traditionally preferred a birch sole, or bottom, rather than the tougher hickory, not only because it weighs less, but also because it is more porous and holds pine tar and wax better.

Wood ski bottoms. (Left to right) Bla-Skia, a racing ski, birch with lignostone edge; Bonna 1800, a light touring ski, hickory with lignostone edge; Bonna 2400, a touring ski, hickory with lignostone edge; Norge-Ski, a mountaineering ski, hickory with steel edge. Note how the width increases with the heavier use of the ski.

Though traditionalists will lament its passing, the all-wood ski is living on borrowed time—probably no more than five years. The racer has largely abandoned it; for him, the finer skiing qualities of the new synthetics have already triggered the switch.

Wood skis with synthetic bottoms. Most of today's synthetic bottoms employ plastic resins or epoxies; some are separate layers bonded to the wood sole, while others are simply special impregnations of that wood. At their best, these are already superior to either hickory or birch in that they do not soak up any water (which would make for a heavier ski). In addition, they are at least as tough as all-wood skis, and they do not require pine tarring. One disadvantage of some of these synthetic bases is that they cannot be heated; this can make cleaning off old waxes rather a chore. Another is that they tend not to hold wax as well.

Synthetic skis. Most major manufacturers now have at least one synthetic racing ski near or at the top of their lines. Some of these have foam or wood cores with a fiber glass wrap; some are "sandwich" fiber glass laminates; one has an aluminum honeycomb core, and others are bound to appear. Some of these still have their bugs; but given early performances, and the remarkable technological progress both American and European manufacturers have made in alpine ski design, the prospect for improved, non-wood touring models has to be bright.

Already the synthetic ski is usually lighter than its wood counterpart, and also nearly indestructible; in addition, exponents point out, the structural properties of glass—its torsion and flex—can be controlled more precisely than those of wood.

ANATOMY OF THE TOURING SKI

From the outside the skis may look simple, but inside it's another story. These cross-sectional diagrams are broadly representative of today's touring ski construction. Note that the stronger, load-bearing materials (especially hickory and fiber glass) lie on, or just beneath, the top and bottom of the ski, while the interior members are lighter and allow for appropriate flexibility.

ALL WOOD

Landsem Deluxe
(light touring)

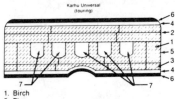

B	B	H	B	H	B	B
B		B		B		B
B	S		S		S	B
L	H	H		H	H	H	L

B — Birch   H — Hickory
S — Spruce   L — Lignostone

WOOD WITH SYNTHETIC BOTTOM

Splitkein Splitkana
(light touring and touring)

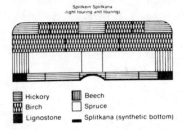

▦ Hickory   ▥ Beech
▨ Birch   ☐ Spruce
■ Lignostone   ▬ Splitkana (synthetic bottom)

WOOD- FIBER GLASS LAMINATE

Karhu Universal
(touring)

1. Birch
2. Pine
3. Hardwood edge
4. Fiber glass laminations (reinforcing)
5. Polyurethane coating
6. Epoxy resin/cellulose fiber synthetic bottom and top
7. Hollow air channels

FIBER GLASS LAMINATE AND WRAP

Rossignol Horizon
(light touring)

1. ABS Plastic top sheet
2. 3. Fiber glass top layers
4. Fiber glass wrap
5. Acrylic foam core
6. ABS Plastic sidewall and edge
7. 8. Fiber glass bottom layers
9. Special ABS Plastic bottom

Presently, only these finer properties need ironing out, and that is coming fast.

A person can travel through unbroken snow on racing skis, but, because they are narrow, such skis sink down and are quite tiring. Don't buy racing skis unless you plan to race, or unless you enjoy running a race course for fun and on high-performance skis. In Scandinavia, especially, a surprising quantity of top grade racing models are sold to non-racers who feel that the ultimate touring thrill is working out with racing skis on a well-groomed track.

Poles

Weight and flexibility are vital. The racing pole ought to have good spring; this helps propel the skier forward in much the same manner as a fiber glass pole whips the vaulter over the bar. For years, all racing poles were made of high-grade bamboo (most notably Tonkin cane); its combination of strength and flexibility were unmatched. More recently manufacturers—especially Scott USA and Liljedahl—have developed light aluminum alloy poles with equal properties. Fiber glass models are also coming onto the market, but break about as easily as cane.

The ring, or basket, on racing poles is small (about 4¼ inches in diameter), because the racer is running entirely on a ready-made trail with a solid pole track. He doesn't have to worry about driving his poles deep into soft, unbroken snow.

As on all poles, an adjustable strap is a must to insure the same correct grip whether one is wearing thin gloves or heavier mitts.

Boots

The racing boot resembles a track shoe, cut below the ankle, with a flexible molded polyurethane (hard rubber) sole. The boot must be as light as possible. There is little need for lateral (or steering) support when the skis stay in a ready-made track.

Bindings

The *rottefella* type toe binding is standard; again, the lighter the better. The entire principle of this binding is over fifty years old and delightfully simple. The unit consists of a metal plate with a flange on either side to hold the boot firmly in place. A row of vertical, ¼-inch pins (the standard number is three) projects up from the base of the plate; these match holes drilled in the sole of the boot. One of a variety of clamps, or bales, is attached toward the front of the plate.

The unit works very simply: you set your toe snugly between the flanges and the pins into the holes; then you clamp the binding in place. That's all. The toe binding allows maximum freedom of movement so the racer can lift his heel easily as he runs.

The *rottefella* type of binding is the foremost racing binding now in use; it is also very popular for light touring. The

Two toe bindings often used by racers or light tour skiers. Note the three pins on each.

word, *rottefella*, is Swedish and translates as "rat trap", an apt description of how this binding works! The Rottefella brand, plus the various Snabb, Troll, Villom, and Karhu models are all sound units.

LIGHT SKI TOURING EQUIPMENT

The difference between racing and light ski touring equipment is merely a matter of degree, and the same is true as we proceed to the equipment used by the tour skier and the ski mountaineer. As the demands of the activity increase, the equipment must be stronger, tougher, and heavier.

Skis

The light touring ski is wider, 50 to 53 millimeters (about 2 inches) and also heavier, about 3½ to 4 pounds. The extra width gives the skier more flotation to keep him from sinking in when he moves into unbroken snow; the extra weight comes from the width and, in the case of wood skis, from two basic differences in construction.

First, on touring skis, the interior balsa laminations and the hollow core are usually replaced by spruce—still a light, flexible wood, but adding substantial strength. Second, the sole of the all wood light touring ski is hickory, a heavier, denser wood that will stand a good deal more wear and tear than the birch bottoms of its racing counterpart. The light tour skier wants this greater strength in his skis; hickory does not hold wax as well as birch, but if it wears off, one can always apply more at his leisure.

A third feature of almost all wood light touring skis is the lignostone edge, which keeps wood from splintering and bruising because of occasional encounters with rocks, ice, hard-crusted snow, etc. Lignostone is not stone at all, but rather beech soaked in a preparation of tars and oils and then hot-compressed to about one-seventh of its original volume. Manufacturers have tried to improve on this edge with various plastics, but so far have failed. Even after its compression, the lignostone retains the basic properties of wood, which means it flexes the same and bonds firmly to the adjoining lamination. A synthetic that behaves as well has yet to be invented.

A word about laminations. Some people would have you believe that the more strips and layers of wood, the better the ski. This just isn't so. The Norwegians and Finns, especially, have been making skis for years, and their experience has led them to the time-tested 16 to 32 laminations for the all-wood ski. This number provides the optimum blend of strength, flexibility, and weight. Fewer laminations make a ski that is too weak, too stiff, or too apt to warp; more do not make much difference at all.

Light touring skis with synthetic bottoms or of glass construction are now fairly well distributed on the market. Even a confirmed wood ski manufacturer, like Norway's Bonna, admits that the competition has forced them to develop a glass ski.

The better of these models often borrow heavily from racing ski technology. The strength of the fiber glass laminates helps make it possible to retain those hollow air channels in a heavier duty ski; this, in turn reduces its weight. The more one travels off the beaten path, the more he will also appreciate the greater durability of fiber glass skis; breaking a tip is still possible, but highly unlikely. The French Rossignol touring skis have gone a step beyond fiber glass—adding a rubberized element into the tips for even greater insurance against breaking. You can lay these skis on the floor, stomp the tips flat, and they'll spring back.

A third major selling point is the convenience of the synthetic bottom. Pine tarring is out, eliminating that maintenance factor altogether. Waxing, however, can be more or less significant depending on the quality of the base; unlike racing skis, which are almost always top-of-the-line, some of the less expensive light touring skis may have inferior bottoms that hold waxes poorly.

Poles

The racing pole is designed for flexibility; all other poles are stiffer, sturdier, and about the same. The basket is larger, about 5 to 5½ inches in diameter, so that the pole will sink less easily into unbroken snow. Metal or Tonkin cane will do the job; the latter used to be less expensive, but materials shortages have

Touring poles have slightly bent tips so they won't jam in the snow.

recently boosted the price. Beware of cheap bamboo, which sometimes splits easily, and can leave one awkwardly without a pole when far from home.

When buying poles, don't be alarmed by the slightly bent tip. It's deliberate, and intended to keep the poles from becoming jammed in the snow every time they're set.

Bindings

The true light touring binding does not exist on today's market. The ideal would be a design that allows the freedom of the toe binding, coupled with the firm boot grip of the cable unit. Beginners sometimes tend to come out of toe bindings, and some could use more lateral support as well.

Toe bindings, however, are what's available. The best bet is to get one of the heavier, more durable models. The sturdier *rottefella* units are as good as any.

In this world of ours that is obsessed with convenience, ingenious equipment inventors have inevitably come up with a toe binding that requires no bending or stooping to clamp or unclamp the boot. The job is done instead with a poke of the tip of the pole. These work well enough, but since bending or stooping on touring skis is almost as easy as doing it barefoot, the convenience is largely superfluous unless you're carrying a heavy pack.

Though not an integral part of the binding, a heel plate or "popper" is a small, but very handy, piece of equipment that belongs on any ski. It's a piece of metal with upturned, sawtooth edges and what looks like a slice off a rubber ball in the middle. This combination of sawtooth edge and rubber "popper" prevents the heel from slipping around on the ski, and snow from building up under the heel. At $1.00 to $1.50 a pair, these handy devices are a bargain.

Boots

The light touring boot is generally cut at mid-ankle, and it is heavier than the boot the racers wear. The first importance of this added strength is greater lateral support (the boot always contributes more to this than the binding). The light touring boot may well be lined for added warmth, and may also have a cushion collar around the ankle and heel to keep out snow. Racers have no need for warmth since they generate plenty of heat on their own. But the light tourer will inevitably stop on the trail to rest, to chat with his companions, or just to look around; at these moments he will welcome the added snugness of a lined boot. The collar is optional; a good pair of gaiters will do a better job of keeping out the snow.

Most boots have leather uppers that are injection-welded onto the polyurethane sole. Rubber or plastic uppers do not usually breathe well; they can readily result in cold, clammy feet and ruin an otherwise fine tour.

TOUR SKIING EQUIPMENT

Four or five years ago, when touring first started to gain popularity here in the United States, most people were going the tour skiing route. That was before most of the areas had developed their trail systems, before the popularity of the citizens' races, and before the perfection of lightweight equipment had accelerated the swing to light touring.

There's no doubt that touring equipment is heavier, which might be a deterrent to some skiers. However, with the growing enthusiasm for wilderness recreation (particularly in the Rockies and the Far West), and with the natural desire of beginning light tourers to extend their skills, there's every chance that tour skiing will soon enjoy a marked recovery of interest and participation.

Skis

The tour ski is wider (54 to 60 mm or 2¼ inches) and heavier (up to 5 pounds) than the light touring ski for the same reasons that the latter is wider and heavier than the racing ski: better flotation on fresh snow, and more strength for traveling in rougher country. For anyone traveling with a backpack or even a heavy rucksack, this extra width can make the difference between a pleasant and a grueling day.

Poles

These are identical to those for light ski touring.

Bindings

Bindings are a subject of much debate. Many tour skiers will go with a cable rather than a toe binding; the weight is greater, but the gain in strength and support is usually worth it. These cable units consist of a flanged plate that blocks in the toe and a cable that reaches around the heel. When this cable is tightened by a clamp attached to the ski 6 or 8 inches in front of the toe plate, the boot is drawn firmly in place, while the heel still has moderate freedom to lift off the ski. The Jofa Cortina is a standard brand.

The greater steering support around the heel can be particularly helpful when making downhill turns, as one would on alpine skis. However, a fair number of tour skiers are making it just fine with the stronger toe bindings and good strong boots.

A typical cable binding used in tour skiing.

HOW TOURING SKIS VARY:
WEIGHT AND WIDTH

The variation among touring skis used for different purposes is both considerable and surprising. The weights listed on this chart are for pairs of skis 200 cm long. The skis listed are quality wood models, except for the Fischer Europa Racing and Europa 77 (fiber glass sandwich), the Fischer Europa (aluminum sandwich), and the Karhu skis (two layers, top and bottom of fiber glass reinforcement).

Make/Model	Weight	Width
Racing Models		
Landsem Lett Racer	45 oz.	46 mm.
Karhu Fiber Racer	46	46
Fischer Europa Racing	52	47
Bla Skia	56	46
Light Touring Skis		
Landsem Standard	62	50
Karhu Universal	62	49
Landsem Deluxe	63	50
Madshus Birkebeiner	68	51
Fischer Europa	68	50
Bonna 1800	72	51
Asnes Langrenn	74	50
Bonna 2000	80	52
Touring Skis		
Karhu Touring	60	54
Fischer Europa 77	80	55
Asnes Touring	84	54
Trysil Knut Marius	85	57
Bonna 2400	90	57
Mountaineering Ski		
Bonna Mountain Blue	112	60

(Courtesy Holubar Mountaineering, Boulder, Colorado and Gerry/Nordic, Denver, Colorado)

Boots

Touring boots are sturdier, and also higher, than light touring boots. They are usually cut right above the ankle. This latter feature gives still greater lateral support and adds its bit of warmth as well. Some touring boots are now being made with synthetic fleece linings; the purpose is greater warmth, but if this lining gets at all wet, the gain rapidly becomes a loss. The fleece also dries very slowly. Heavy socks are a better bet . here—an extra pair in the pack will always be both warm and bone dry.

SKI MOUNTAINEERING EQUIPMENT

Once again the weight increases. Skiing in severe alpine conditions—on steep slopes, covered by snow that is deep and windpacked hard—requires heavy, durable equipment.

Skis

Today, most mountaineering skis are like downhill skis were 20 years ago: stiff wooden models with steel edges. The bottoms must be tough—hickory or synthetic. Above all, the mountaineering ski must be strong; to break a ski when five days from civilization is to court danger.

Poles

Good, strong, light touring poles will do the job for the ski mountaineer. Some prefer the even stiffer alpine poles for the long, downhill runs that can be so much a part of this sport.

Bindings

For most ski mountaineers, standard cable bindings are more than adequate. With a toe binding, one could not sufficiently control the heavy skis; the hard twisting and torque in the toe plate would soon break the boot apart or at least weaken it considerably. Some ski mountaineers might be tempted to go another step to specialized alpine touring bindings. They perform the dual task of leaving the heel free for travel on the flat and uphill, while anchoring it to the ski for the descent. Of these, the Silvretta models are the most popular—still a cable binding, but with a hinged toe plate that allows unlimited heel lift without the boot sole itself flexing. For the descent, the cable is simply hitched down to catches back near the heel on either side of the ski.

This type of binding should be regarded with extreme caution; lacking a reliable safety release, it has been dubiously dubbed the "bear-trap" binding, because there is little to give (except a bone in the leg) in case of a severe, twisting fall. Far into the wilderness, running such a risk is not worth it. If you need a toe-hinge binding, fine. Just don't hitch it down unless the ski patrol is near. The top-of-the-line Silvretta, the Remy Securus, and several new step-in-type alpine touring bindings do have adequate safety releases; these are normally available only in the more specialized ski mountaineering shops, and are very expensive—between $30 and $80.

A far better and more economical solution is simply to stick with the standard cable binding and to improve your skiing ability to the point where this model is all you need. Since well-executed modern downhill technique generally leaves your weight well back on the ski, this is not as implausible a suggestion as it might seem.

Boots

These must be firm and roomy without being loose; the heel fit must be solid, the sole usually stiff. The usual cut is 8 or 9 inches, like an ordinary work boot, while the tougher all-around construction provides optimum lateral support. A solid, well-made pair of summertime mountain climbing boots (with a notch cut in the heel for the cable) will work well here, as will those now old-fashioned leather, lace-type alpine ski boots that can often be salvaged from the nearest attic. As with the fleece-lined touring boots, surplus lining here may be great

Touring boots. (Left to right) ski mountaineering boot, 9-inch cut; touring boot, cut above the ankle; light touring boot, cut across the ankle; racing boot, cut below the ankle.

for warmth, but watch out when it gets wet.

So there you have it; all touring equipment varies from the ultralight to the heavy, from the extremely flexible to the fairly stiff, from that which provides very little support to that which is firm. The choice is yours.

THE MOST COMMON EQUIPMENT QUESTIONS

Now you're ready to head for the store—almost. There are still some important odds and ends of information you need to know. Two cardinal points should be noted before you even enter a store. First, choose your equipment for the *dominant use* you anticipate. If light touring is your goal, but you've a yen for unbroken snow on occasion, buy light touring gear. You can make do with it on the tour skier's trail as well. Second, be sure to *match your equipment.* Don't try to get by with a light touring boot on a touring ski. It's not quite as bad as wearing hiking boots on a tennis court, but the principle is the same. Matched gear will work together smoothly for you.

Where do I buy equipment?

The safest bet is a shop that specializes in touring equipment. In most places this means one of the booming number of backpacking and mountaineering outlets: places that carry sleeping bags, hiking boots, backpacks, freeze-dried foods and related merchandise. Until ski touring came along, many of these shops struggled through the cold months as best they could. Today they are geared into ski touring as the bread and butter of their fall and winter business.

Many traditional ski shops that have catered to downhillers for years now include touring departments. If this section of the store is well staffed and stocked and seems to be a going concern in its own right, it's probably solid. If it's just a sideline to the alpine business, you'd best try elsewhere; your range of choices will be smaller and the sales staff may well be short on know-how.

The latter problem also holds with many of the larger, "discount" sporting goods stores that carry everything from shotguns to fishing plugs in addition to touring equipment. The stock may well be decent enough, but the sales help can leave something to be desired when it comes to responding ably to your questions.

Should I rent equipment?

If you're a bit undecided and want to sample the sport before committing yourself, renting is a reasonable option. Prices are modest; skis, bindings, boots, and poles go for about $6.00 a day. A shop that specializes in touring equipment will usually have rentals.

How much should I spend?

Like the 30-cent gallon of gas, the good old days of the $50 to $70 touring package—skis, poles, boots, bindings—now seem gone forever. The downward fluctuating American dollar is not the only cause of this. The sudden growth of the touring sport has placed a severe strain on the supply of some materials, causing prices to skyrocket. Hickory, for example, is acutely scarce, which is one of the main reasons why the cost of all-wood skis continues to rise so sharply. Raw leather prices tripled from 1972 to 1974, mainly because of shortages of Argentine, Brazilian, and Austrian hides; boot consumers must inevitably foot much of this bill.

Equally significant, however, are those increased costs resulting from improved touring equipment technology. The relatively new aluminum alloy poles are tougher than their bamboo predecessors, but they are also more expensive. The same is true of the synthetic bottoms on wood skis, and even more of the increasingly specialized fiber glass skis. With each the quality improves, but so does the cost.

With these varied increases, current price ranges (mid-1970s) for sound, reliable recreational touring equipment look like this. You can find models both above and below these prices; buy the more expensive if you wish, but avoid the cheaper as they're too apt to be inferior.

Wood skis	$42 to $60	racing models
Wood-fiber glass skis	$55 to $90	will cost more
Wood-metal skis	$55 to $90	
Bamboo poles	$6.75 to $10.00	
Metal poles	$7.50 to $25.00	
Fiber glass poles	$10.00 to $15.00	
Boots	$27.50 to $50.00	
Toe bindings	$6.50 to $10.00	
Cable bindings	$8.00 to $12.00	

The best advice is to buy *now*. These prices will continue to rise; the longer you wait, the more you will pay. Low cost is no longer the open door to touring, as it was in the early 1970s; however, the price break, when compared to downhill skiing, is still significant (top-of-the-line alpine skis are actually closing in on $300, while boots are nudging $200).

For bargain hunters, a few avenues still remain open. Buying a complete touring package (skis, boots, bindings, poles, sometimes a wax kit, plus a labor charge for mounting the bindings) usually saves about 20 percent. If you're a confirmed opportunist and don't mind buying in the off-season, try hitting a touring shop when it's selling off the previous winter's rental stock. For a few scratches and scuff marks, you can often save 30 to 50 percent.

Wood or glass?

By the end of the 1970s, the all-wood ski will probably have departed the way of the dodo. The growing superiority of synthetic and fiber glass technology is the most obvious reason for this. Equally important are the spiralling costs of raw woods—especially hardwoods—and their impact on ski prices. Most observers in the mid-seventies are quick to point out that these costs are rising at a rate faster than normal inflation; they also foresee a time very soon when fiber glass touring ski technology will be automated to the point that prices for these skis will remain fairly steady—or perhaps even drop. Thus, the demise of the all-wood ski will also be a matter of economics; as soon as it is both outperformed and underpriced by its synthetic competitors, it will have no other choice than to phase out.

Only that elusive thing called taste might partially check this trend. A finely crafted all-wood ski, like the Madshus Birkebeiner, is a thing of beauty; its hand-rubbed hickory finish seems the very embodiment of tradition in a sport whose roots sink 4,500 years into the past; it is also a quality light touring ski in its own right. Its continued existence on the market will depend on strong public demand despite a price that is bound to increase. Tour skiers have already proven an unusually independent lot, so the exact direction here is hard to predict.

What about ski length?

There are no hard and fast rules about ski length; world championships have been won on 180-cm skis, and they have been won on 240-cm skis. Some short people prefer long skis, while some tall people prefer shorter skis. There is no universal prescription.

For someone starting out, the general rule of thumb is this: Stand straight and reach directly up with your arm; then bend your wrist at a right angle. At that point, you should be just touching the tip of the ski that "fits" you.

For many people, a shorter ski is more maneuverable, especially in making turns. On the other hand, a longer ski tends to follow the track more easily. This varies considerably from one individual to the next. Start out using the general rule of thumb and you'll be close enough. When you move on to a second pair of skis, you can adjust to longer or shorter models according to your experience and ability. Many people do not change at all.

What about camber?

Camber is the noticeable, arching bend in each ski, most visible as you sight along it from tip to tail. All skis have camber. The principle is this: when you stand in the middle of the ski, your weight will be distributed evenly along its entire length. With too much camber, the tips and tails will dig into the snow and slow you down; with too little, the ski will tend to pivot around its center and be hard to steer. For racers, slight variations in camber can be critical factors affecting their speed; for all others, it is less important, as most skis are designed to handle weights well to either side of the average. Only if you are exceptionally heavy or light should you pay special attention to camber.

Should my skis have special bottoms?

In many shops you'll discover one or more skis with specially designed bottoms: fishscales, grooved steps or parallel mohair strips. A few of these rate some comment.

The Trak ski's fishscale bottom looks just like that; think of a good largemouth bass and you'll have the picture. The idea is that you can slide forward with the scales, and won't slip back against them. Advertisements bill these as "no wax—no slip" skis, and under most conditions, this is true. What is also true is that they do not usually glide well either, which means more work on the flat and slower running down hills. Since most touring trails have their share of gentle slopes, this can be a drawback. The ladder-like grooves in the base of Fischer's Europa Step ski work similarly to the fishscale, but generally give a better glide. Only the absolute beginner who doesn't want to wax or who is afraid of slipping or sliding needs these special bottoms; others may use them if they prefer.

Skis with parallel mohair or synthetic fiber strips running along the bottom for three feet or so under the boot employ the same principle. You slide forward with the grain of the fur and don't slip back against it. You also add a slight drag on the flat or going downhill. Though most manufacturers have now added a "no wax" mohair strip ski to their lines, the same advice applies here as for the fishscales.

Manufacturers are continuing to work on improving all these special bottoms and devising new ones; there is bound to be some progress made in the future.

What is the best pole length?

Here's a firm rule: When you're standing straight, the pole, from tip to top, should reach to a point midway between your shoulder and your armpit. Out in the snow, a pole that is too long or too short will hinder your technique. Be precise.

Racers are the only exception here. For them, pole length can vary considerably, depending on the track, strength in the arms, and other factors.

How do I know a boot fits?

A touring boot must fit well. If it does not, the result will be aching feet, or blisters, or both. Do your trying on with the socks you plan to wear; for most people that means a heavy wool sock over a light cotton or cotton-synthetic one. The fit should be like a good street shoe. Be sure the heel is snug; if it isn't, you're just asking for blisters. You should also have room for wiggling your toes a bit; this helps keep your feet warm on cold days and avoids that jammed, pinched feeling.

Most touring boots marketed in the United States today are made in Europe, which means the sizes are marked according to the European system. Thus, when the salesman tells you to take a size 42, don't be confused; it's really a man's 8½. All properly managed shops have size conversion charts to unravel these mysteries.

Width is standard for every size; there are no AAA's or EEE's. If you encounter problems here, two solutions exist: shop for a make of boot that is wider (or narrower), or, less preferably, since most boots tend to lean toward the wide side, compensate with an extra pair of socks.

Lightweight rubber boot gloves are invaluable in wet snow.

If you anticipate much of any skiing in wet snow conditions, by all means plunk down an extra $3.00 or $3.50 for a pair of boot gloves. Made of lightweight quality rubber, these fit tightly over the boot; on a wet day, they'll keep your boot dry. They're also eminently practical around a campfire where the snow often tends to become slushy.

How do I choose a rucksack?

If you plan to tour out of sight of civilization, a rucksack is important. You'll need something for carrying an extra sweater, socks, wax, your lunch, and a number of other items (these depend on the extent of your wanderings; for a detailed discussion, see Chapter 6). Every major manufacturer of backpacking equipment has at least one rucksack in its line; some have over a dozen. These place a little added weight on your shoulders, but the better models have waist straps to anchor the sack and keep it from flopping around on your back. For day tours, ample packs are available that weigh less than a pound when empty. Larger models go up to three pounds, but unless you need the added room, there's no point in carrying the extra weight. Be sure the fabric is waterproof, as there's every chance it will end up in the snow a time or two.

For short tours through familiar terrain, the rucksack can give way to the fanny pack, which straps around the waist. A fanny pack is small, but sufficient to carry the minimal gear you'll need.

What is the best type of clothing for touring?

The first rule for ski touring dress is: make sure it's comfortable. The second is: use the *layer principle*. You do not want anything that will hamper your movement; you do want to dress so that you can regulate your body temperature. That's where the layer principle comes in. Ski touring can be very much a hot and cold activity. When you start out first thing in the morning, the temperature will be low and you won't be warmed up. As the day progresses and you get rolling, it can seem almost like summer. When you take a break for lunch and stop working, chances are you'll grow chilly. Then comes the hot afternoon sun. The cycle continues.

The ideal is to dress so you're warm but not so you overheat and thereby risk becoming badly chilled when the wind picks up or you stop for a rest. Dressing in layers allows you to add or shed clothing according to your needs. A combination of comparatively thin layers—long underwear or a cotton turtleneck (not nylon; it breathes poorly), a shirt, a light sweater, a medium sweater, and a windbreaker—will usually do the job. For the legs, some people will want to apply the layer principle in the form of cross-country warm-up pants or extra long gaiters. There are infinite variations on these generalizations. Only the windbreaker (with a hood and drawstring) is essential in case you encounter sudden wind, storm, or cold.

Another important point: the person who stays dry stays warm. Select clothing that sheds the snow. Do not overdress—perspiration can readily turn to a severe, penetrating chill.

A few don'ts are worth noting:

• Don't wear a quilted parka (down, for example) or a heavy jacket. The layer principle requires that you take off or add a small bit at a time; these thick, bulky units are too much.

• Don't wear blue jeans. They are very absorbent, get wet quickly, and then freeze stiff like cardboard. This makes them both awkward and extremely cold. Corduroy is only slightly better. A baggy, wool pant is excellent, which is why knickers are so popular. Chances are you have a perfectly decent pair of touring pants hanging in the back of your closet right now; if not, try the Salvation Army, Goodwill, or their kin. Long underwear is handy on cold or windy days.

• Don't wear downhill-type stretch pants; they hinder your freedom of movement. Every time you stride, you are working against the fabric; the effort may be infinitesimal by itself, but multiply it a thousandfold (you'll take that many strides on even a comparatively short tour), and the added labor mounts up. Anything you wear should be loose enough to provide full freedom of movement.

The choice of mittens or gloves depends on both you and the weather. Mittens are usually considered warmer, but they can hinder your handling of the poles. Cold hands can make a day miserable, so it's best to err on the side of caution.

Since up to 60 percent of the body's heat can be lost through the head, a warm (not hot) hat is essential. A wool pullover-style that covers your ears when it's cold does the job as well as any. In the spring, a brimmed model (variations here are infinite and whimsical) cuts down on the glare.

A final refinement is the gaiter. This is a tube-like, water-proofed piece of cloth that is pulled around the lower leg, secured tightly over the shoe top (usually with laces that run under the boot), and pulled as high as it goes. There are ankle-length gaiters, knee-length gaiters, and several sizes in between. They're invaluable for keeping snow from sifting or trickling down into your boots and chilling your feet in a hurry; gaiters also keep snow from sticking to wool socks and provide an extra layer of insulation. The length depends on the snow depth you plan to ski through.

TAKING CARE OF YOUR EQUIPMENT

When well cared for, good touring equipment will last a number of years—even if heavily used. A few simple do's and don'ts will handle this one.

Skis

The newer plastic-metal combination models are highly dura-ble and need little attention, though the synthetic bottoms should be checked periodically. Deep scratches and gouges should be fixed with do-it-yourself kits, which are available for most bottoms (if not, then don't buy that particular ski). Wood skis are a different matter, though proper care is no great chore.

First of all, watch the bottoms; be sure they are well tarred or impregnated (for a full discussion of pine tar, see Chapter 5) so they won't soak up any measurable amounts of water. Bare hickory will do this and even the toughest fibers will tear and rough up when wet. The result is a heavy, dragging ski. It's wise to check your bottoms fairly regularly, and not just before you head off into the snow and there's no time for tarring. If the wood is getting at all light in color, add a fresh coat. There's no need for sanding unless you wish to smooth out some scratches or abrasions; use fine sandpaper for this.

Second, don't store your skis in snowbanks. With wood skis, especially, avoid extreme changes in temperature when you take them inside. A difference of 30 or 40 degrees can cause sudden and disastrous warping, or less seriously, a change in the camber, which could markedly impair the performance of the ski. The garage, basement, or shed are the best spots for all skis—the drier the better.

Note: Sometimes new wood skis tend to be slightly dry and brittle. A brief breaking in, which means modest skiing on moderate terrain, is wise. The converse of this is: don't go jumping fences or ditches on brand new skis. Like good wine, a well-cared-for pair of wood skis will improve with age— becoming marvelously flexible, loose, and superior to most skis you could ever buy in a store.

Boots

If you own a pair of hiking boots, then you probably know how to take care of touring boots. Keep them well treated, but don't overdo it, and above all, don't saturate the leather (you'll make it heavier and reduce its insulating properties). Unless you're skiing in lots of wet mush, you'll probably treat only twice or three times a year. The best time to do this is after the boots have been used and are wet, but almost dried out (at room temperature and no more). It pays to work and knead the compound vigorously into the leather with your hands; a light daubing is not enough. Mink oil or the synthetic Sno-Seal are the standard preparations for boot care; you won't go wrong with either.

That's it for equipment. Touring is a simple sport and so, basically, is its equipment. Don't make it any more complex than you have to. Get sensibly outfitted; then forget about it and have fun.

3

Instruction

Ski touring technique involves only a very few skills; but they are essential, and learning them at the outset is bound to make the sport more enjoyable for years to come. Thus, it's best to start out with a lesson or two, maybe three —but seldom any more, because there just isn't that much to teach. After that it's simply a matter of practice; with a little diligence, you'll find yourself improving as you go along.

Instructors differ in their approach to touring just as they do with any other activity. However, the basics of ski touring are so elementary that the variation in approaches is apt to be considerably less than in most other sports.

FIRST LESSON

This will normally take place on a prepared loop-type track that's pretty much on the flat. The lesson shouldn't last beyond an hour and a half to two hours at the most. In this session, you should learn and practice the basic level ground turns, how to

35

fall down and get up, and, most important, the basic striding and poling techniques (these are explained in detail in Chapter 4).

SECOND LESSON

This time, the instructor will move you to a modest hill where you'll learn about climbing and coming down (these are also explained in detail in Chapter 4). The latter will involve the various downhill turns. This should take about the same amount of time as the first lesson.

That's all there is to it; the rest is practice.

Before, between, or after these lessons (usually the earlier the better), a good instructor will throw in an indoor session for discussion of equipment, waxing, and other elements of the sport. If the facilities exist, he or she might show you a short touring film or screen some slides. Much of this material can be worked into the two basic touring lessons, but this can also lead to a torrent of information that is hard to assimilate in a single gulp.

Many lodges and touring centers offer advanced lessons as well. In some cases these will be on the track where the emphasis is on refining technique both for racers and non-racers. In other instances advanced lessons will consist of relatively short tours with instruction along the way as the terrain dictates.

COMPETENT INSTRUCTION—WHERE TO FIND IT

When the ski touring boom first hit the United States five or six years ago, skilled instructors were in critically short supply. Beginners simply went out, bought the equipment, and stumbled off on their own like backpackers or rockhounds. Others, with a more entrepreneuring bent, set themselves up as instructors without really understanding the dimensions of this sport; more than a few people were duped.

Today this situation is changed. Across the United States, various regional ski touring associations and councils have established certification programs for instructors. By this method the sport is progressively purging itself of those hacks who took advantage of the initial boom. Thus, the general rule for the beginner today is to seek out a certified instructor. These are not hard to find; most major downhill ski areas have one or more instructors on their permanent staff, or else are closely affiliated with some. In addition, numerous lodges and resorts, not involved in the downhill sport, now have developed touring programs.

If you have trouble tracking down a certified instructor, inquire at your regional touring association or council (see Appendix A for a list of these).

A good instructor does not necessarily have to be certified, but a certified instructor is usually able. Though the programs vary from region to region, all strive to have only skilled, knowledgeable, and sensible people teaching the sport.

In the Rockies, for example, the certifying agency is the Rocky Mountain Ski Instructors Association, headquartered in Steamboat Springs, Colorado. This group's program requires attendance at an intensive instructors' clinic prior to a stiff two-day examination. In order to pass (and in 1974 only 30 percent did), the candidate must demonstrate knowledge, competence and the ability to teach the following:

- Equipment and clothing
- Ski touring technique
- Waxing
- Tour leadership (doing this well requires a combination of common sense, perception and patience in addition to the more obvious skills and knowledge)
- Use of map and compass (so one can find one's way around in the mountains)
- First aid (an American Red Cross Advanced First Aid and Emergency Care Card is required)
- Winter survival
- Snow conditions and avalanches
- Provisioning a tour

There's plenty of detail packed into each of these categories, and it's well impossible to bluff one's way through all of them. After one passes, he must then serve a period of apprenticeship before full certification.

Another, and often more convenient source of instruction, is the backpacking-ski touring specialty shops where you most likely will buy your equipment. A number of these outlets offer free evening clinics (movies, tips on equipment, technique, waxing, etc.) to customers—both actual and potential. These sessions can be a handy way for the beginner to get at least a preliminary taste of the sport. Some of these shops also have their own certified instructors and offer lessons as well as organized group tours ("We'll go every Sunday while the snow lasts," reads a brochure from one of Denver's better touring shops).

LESSONS—WHAT THEY COST

Prices of lessons vary, but none can be considered expensive. The usual cost of a group lesson (seldom more than ten people; above that it gets unwieldy and the individual tends to become lost in the crowd) ranges between $5.00 and $8.00 for 90 minutes out in the snow. Private lessons run from $10.00 to $15.00. Since you need only a couple of these, the investment is small and well worth every penny.

TEACHING CHILDREN

Dr. Spock has never written a word on touring, but his style of wisdom is wonderfully apt for this sport. Any child can be given a pair of skis not long after he or she learns to walk. Packaged sets (skis, poles and step-in leather strap bindings that fit regular overshoes) are available for about $20. If the parents ski at all, the interest will be spontaneous and enthusiastic. Do not try to force an interest.

The typical two-year-old will do all sorts of wonderfully irrelevant things with a pair of skis—lie on them, sit on them, dig with them, play with them like any other wood toy. One day, however, he will discover that the most efficient way to use them, for getting around, is to slide along like Mommy and Daddy. Waiting for that day can be frustrating. The obvious temptation is to push or instruct; this usually stifles the child's natural inclinations. Let your child work it out at his own pace; he has all kinds of years ahead of him and there's no hurry at all.

Starting a child on skis at two or three often has another side benefit. As long as you bundle him well in a warm snowsuit, mittens, and boots (but not so tightly he can barely move), chances are he'll grow up with positive feelings about winter. It's surprising, and a bit sad too, how many American children miss this pleasure.

As the child grows older, you'll see him doing more and more on his skis very naturally. He'll discover that crossing them gets him nowhere; he'll develop methods of getting up (though an occasional helping hand is appreciated); he'll improvise a step turn without a word of instruction from you; and, all the time he'll work out his own senses of balance and coordination—important not only for skiing, but for all activities.

For most children, age eight is early enough for formal touring instruction—if it is wanted at the time. Until then, the best approach is to answer the questions as they're asked. Stamp out a track in the yard if you have room (tracks are fun to follow); take time to ski *with* the child so he can watch what you do, and have fun with you too. For the rest, just let his interest and skill happen. Chances are good that it will do just that.

4

Technique

It's often said that touring is an easy sport; this is true. It's also often said that all you must do is buy your equipment and then go touring, which is quite possible. Many beginners take precisely this route, and they're rarely miserable. But although touring can be a pleasant do-it-yourself activity, the sport also has a clearly defined technique, which is based on years of experience. Very simply, it strives for efficiency, ease and grace. Doing it well saves you energy and feels nice, to boot. Doing it very well can be truly blissful. So why not?

Thus the basic approach of this chapter may be summarized as follows: there's not very much to ski touring technique; what little there is you'll find invaluable.

The first point to make after such a statement is: don't be skittish about technique. Don't be self-conscious and worry how you look. In short, relax! Even as you work on and think about your touring technique, remember that enjoyment comes first and foremost.

For reasons that have been explored in some depth by sociologists and psychologists, many people tend to develop sad and unnecessary hang-ups about their form in many sports—and how it impresses others. Perhaps the ethics of competition have something to do with this, but there are other reasons as well. For example, in this country, children growing through the school system tend to learn only specialized skills so they can excel in particular sports. It's pretty much a bits-and-pieces proposition. In the process, they develop precious little general knowledge of how their bodies really work—about such basic things as movement, balance, coordination, timing, reflexes, rhythm, and grace. This is unfortunate, because it often makes learning a new sport a matter of starting completely from scratch. It is also why an American who is, for example, magnificently fluid and powerful on a basketball court can be completely lost on a soccer field, or even on a volleyball court (though that sport is closely related to basketball).

In Scandinavia, this kind of thing rarely happens. Because of gymnastics, which is an integral part of the educational system, the growing child develops a much greater intuitive awareness of what his body can and cannot do—and of how and why it does what it does. Beginning in kindergarten, he will start learning a chain of movements of different parts of his body. All through school this continues; the emphasis is on the body itself—not on its ability to compete with others. By the time a youth reaches college, chances are he will have seen and experienced all the basic movements there are. Even if it's totally unfamiliar in itself, a new movement will be so related to one learned in childhood that mastery will come quickly and with ease. There'll be little need to develop and strengthen new muscles, little difficulty in working out new combinations of balance and coordination.

But why mention this to people first getting into a new sport?

First, perhaps to put you at ease; if you feel a bit awkward flopping around on the skis, don't be concerned; chances are that it's less your problem than it is one of your schooling.

Second, to make a point about touring technique: its movements are simple, basic, essential. Some have called an able tour skier "poetry in motion"; certainly there can be a ballet-like quality to the sport. Touring might actually get you in closer touch with yourself, your body, where it begins and ends and how it works.

Or finally, look at it in a third way. Touring technique is an extension of one of the most essential movements you know: walking. In touring, that basic walk takes on a few modest embellishments that enable you to *glide* rather than just stride along. That's all.

So much for all the philosophy you're going to get. The rest of this chapter will talk about the basics of technique for the tour skier, not the racer. If you're interested in getting into the competitive end of this sport, technique will mean careful, patient refining of these basics. You might want to buy a book such as John Caldwell's warm and lucid *The New Cross-Country Skiing Book* (Brattleboro, VT: 1973), which is well packed with accurate information on racing technique—no more than an extension of that used in touring, with a few different points of emphasis.

TECHNIQUE EXERCISES

To begin, if you're going to use this book to teach yourself technique, find a small practice track on the flat. If you can't find one, make one yourself; just ski over the same loop trail two or three times until the track is firm. Your track does not have to be long; a loop 50 yards from end to end is plenty. This will give you something solid to ski on and you won't have to worry about obstacles. Furthermore, try starting out under the best possible conditions; good snow, the proper wax, and pleasant weather allow you to concentrate wholly on yourself and the skis.

The following series of technique exercises are designed specifically to develop those parts of the body you'll use in tour skiing technique. General relaxation, strength in the legs, flexibility in the shoulders, an overall sense of balance—do not confuse these with technique itself. The principle here is of emphasis; the intent is to help you develop individual muscles, ligaments, or movements you'll use later on when you're out touring by focusing your efforts on them now. Basic conditioning, which strengthens the working capacity of the lungs and heart, is a different process.

These exercises are not touring technique itself; rather they are a kind of preface aimed at getting you into it. Treat them as a pleasant and useful starter. Do a loop around the track with each and you'll be well warmed up. More important, you'll also have gone through the basic movements—here deliberately exaggerated—that you'll use in all your touring from here on in.

Final note: at this point, your poles will only clutter up what you're trying to work out and feel; set them aside in the snow until later.

Preface: A Relaxed, Upright Position

This is not an exercise, but a vital prelude. It's easy for a first-timer on skis to make the assumption that he'll have to do

The relaxed upright position. Ski this way and you'll burn less energy while travelling both farther and faster.

many new and different things. "It can't be that simple," goes the reasoning; "there's just no way."

In truth, there really is. Try this. If you exclude sitting and lying down, what is the most restful position you can get your body into? The answer: a straight, simple standing position with your weight evenly distributed over both feet. Bending forward requires more effort; so do bent knees. The relaxed upright position is it.

For touring, this is critical. The point, at all times, is to ski in this position, or as close as possible to it. Nothing less will do. One of the prime satisfactions you'll derive from ski touring comes from the fact that, when you do it well, you'll burn less energy while traveling both farther and faster. It's a matter of economy of motion all the way; standing straight on your skis is the most economical thing you can do.

Until it becomes intuitive, make a deliberate effort to begin everything you do from this relaxed upright position and to stay as close to it as you're reasonably able. This could well be the key to your touring pleasure.

Exercise #1: The Glide (for balance and relaxation)

Good touring technique is easy going—not stiff, not tense, not jerky. Use this exercise to ease you into a smooth, relaxed movement.

Start out as if you were just walking in the relaxed upright position; then ease into a glide with each stride. Do not lift the ski as you do this; keep your body straight and your knees bent normally. As your left ski comes forward, keep your weight on it a second or two and let it slide along; as your right comes forward, do likewise. Then as the glide slows, give a slight push or *kick* with that weighted leg; it will increase your forward speed and trigger a weight shift to the opposite ski, which will quickly be gliding along ahead of you. Let your arms hang loosely at your sides; let your legs work the gliding. Do this as effortlessly as you possibly can—no stiffness, no tension,

Exercise #1: The Glide.

all looseness. Try to keep a steady glide-kick-glide rhythm to get the feel of this easy skiing.

Exercise #2: Exaggerated Knee Bend (to build strength)

When you're skiing, your knees should never bend any more than the conditions require; it is hard on your legs and tiring. A degree of knee bend, however, is often necessary for balance and to absorb shock. Sometimes it is very little, for example, when you're coasting down a long, gentle slope. Sometimes it is considerably greater, for example, when climbing a hill, doing a turn, or making a faster downhill run. For situations

Exercise #2: The Exaggerated Knee Bend.

like these, your legs must be strong; the exaggerated knee bend will develop this.

Start out from the relaxed upright position, as you did in the Glide, but now bend your knees as you stride, extending the skis far forward and back. Keep your center of gravity very low as if you were sneaking quickly through a woods; keep your head up and your torso erect. Bend neither forward nor to the side; don't bounce up and down either.

If this exercise tires your legs (particularly your thighs), then you're doing it exactly right. You should be overloading those muscles as you keep your knees bent while gliding.

Exercise #3: Exaggerated Arm Swing (for flexibility)

There's an old adage in touring technique that goes like this: work ahead with your skis, work behind with your poles. The

Exercise #3: The Exaggerated Arm Swing.

concern with the arm is, more specifically, with the even extended follow-through of the poling movement, which should provide measurable forward push and help prevent backsliding.

Again, keep your torso erect and ease into the glide-kick-glide, then into the exaggerated knee bend. This time, however, pretend your arms are loose, flexible pendulums. Emphasize the backswing, the follow back and through (the arms will come forward easily enough). As you do naturally when walking, on skis you'll find that your left arm and right leg will go back together; then your right arm and left leg. Don't try anything one bit less natural; first one arm, then the other should swing back. Shoulders should be loose and flexible.

All forces should be moving back and forth in the same direction you're going; the motion of the arms should be lined up directly with that of the ski. Don't throw the arm out to the side and pull it in either behind or in front.

Again, if the upper arms and shoulders don't become tired, you're not letting the exercise do its job. Overload them. Swing further back. If you don't tire a part of your body, you're not really exercising it.

Exercise #4: Quickski (for balance, endurance, flexibility)

This is a multipurpose exercise that will work on your endurance, the flexibility in your shoulders (again), and your balance. Depending on your pace, the emphasis will differ: do it rapidly and your breathing should increase and your heart start to pump; do it more slowly and you should feel yourself carefully balancing as you ski along.

For the quick version, here's how: bend your arms sharply at the elbows and hook them in close to your sides; as you start glide-kick-gliding in a sharp, quick rhythm, swing your arms from the shoulders in short, compact arcs, being sure to bring them back as far as you can. This arm movement should be similar to that of sprinting, but don't let the analogy carry over to your legs and start trying to run on your skis; they should stay

Exercise #4: The Quickski.

on the snow, moving along in short, stabbing strides. Try also to emphasize the weight shift from ski to ski, without excess rock or sway, in order to work your balance into this act.

To work on your weight shift (i.e., balance), just do the quickski in slow motion. Call this variation the "slow ski" if you must. It should involve a pronounced, graceful, easy exaggeration of the normal glide-kick-glide motion. Imagine you're a figure skater performing to a steady, restrained, almost arrested beat. First glide entirely on one ski, then the other, but don't lift the unweighted ski. To balance more easily, keep the weighted leg slightly bent.

While you're at it, note that this variation is also an exercise in alternating work and rest, a principle that is essential to efficient touring technique. As the left ski glides forward and carries your weight, the right leg should be relaxing in an easy follow-through, which changes into a thrust forward and weighting on it as the left leg follows through, and back, and relaxes. It's often said that the truly effortless skier never works with more than one arm and one leg at a time; the other arm and leg are resting while in a recovering motion.

Consider all of these exercises as the tour skier's special extensions and adaptations of everyday walking or jogging. In doing them, you should, after first relaxing, have exercised yourself into the highest possible gear—first your legs, then your arms, finally your balance. On any normal tour, you will very rarely exert yourself to these extremes; the pieces you have isolated and stressed in these exercises will, like Humpty-Dumpty, be put back together again—all working in concert to make your trip a smoother, more pleasant experience.

TECHNIQUE: ON THE FLAT

Now turn from the technique exercises to technique itself. The purpose of all touring technique is one thing only: ease. You should be able to ski faster, longer, and with less energy. Even this, enjoyable as it may often be, should be no more than a passing end in itself; consider it instead as a means to the true goal of this sport, which is relaxation, fun, and delight in that brave new world of winter.

Most touring takes place on the flat, or on gentle ups and downs; for this kind of terrain, there are only two basic movements, plus a third, which is no more than a combination of the first two. That's all.

The diagonal. This is the basic touring stride; you'll probably use it 75 percent of the time.

The Diagonal

This is the basic touring stride. It is also an inevitably natural stride; even if you took off on your skis with absolutely no prior knowledge of the sport, you'd still fall into some version of the diagonal. There are, however, well-defined ways of doing it that result in greater ease and efficiency; there's little point in charging ahead with the hope that you'll stumble onto them by chance (even though you could get lucky and do it). Another point: out in the snow you'll probably be using the diagonal stride about 75 percent of the time. That in itself is ample reason for learning it well.

For learning the diagonal, you'll want to use your poles, and though it may seem pedantic to go into it, there is only one way these should be held. Reach your hand up through the strap loop and then grip the pole along with the upper end of the strap. You should feel a firmness and support as the loop winds around the back of your hand. Relax your grip and the pole will dangle a bit, but the strap will keep it well within your grasp.

Pole grip. You should feel a firmness and support as the strap loop winds around the back of your hand.

First of all, as you work on the diagonal, it will help to think in terms of the technique exercises you've just been through; doing the diagonal, you'll glide easily, bend your knees as necessary, follow through with your arms, and shift your weight.

Begin the stride itself by easing into the glide-kick-glide motion you've already practiced. The body should be in that relaxed upright position; the knees should bend loosely as you stride ahead first on one ski, then the other. As the left ski comes forward, your right arm will do likewise. Plant the pole so you can use it for push immediately. As your right ski comes forward, let the left arm do likewise. Arms and legs both should work alternately, like relaxed pendulums. Most of the strength that drives you forward will come from your legs, but the poling will provide a noticeable boost, too.

In a nutshell, that is the famous diagonal. Try it slowly around the track. Don't worry about any speed; trying to rush at this point will only foul your coordination. As your technique improves, you'll find that speed comes naturally. For now, work on developing a relaxed, regular rhythm. You may slip a bit here and there, or wobble a little from side to side, but don't worry; as your balance, flexibility, and strength develop, you'll quickly get over both.

Now for some specific pointers:

The Kick. This commonly used term can be confusing on two counts. First, it often conjures up an image of how a punter drives his foot forward into the ball. This is misleading; think instead of how a mule kicks back at something it dislikes. Secondly, only the racer truly kicks—to increase his speed. For most recreational skiers, the term pushoff is more accurate and applicable to what his legs are doing in the diagonal stride.

Only two basic points need to be made here. First, be sure your weight shift is complete before you begin to push off (or kick). Secondly, begin that pushoff early, when your leg is under, or even a little ahead, of your body. Sometimes it actually helps to think of this as a pull-push motion, since physically you cannot start the kick until your leg is beneath you; by pulling the leg back prior to the kick, you're sure to begin it early. Both points are very important. Neither movement comes naturally to most beginning skiers; often they do not complete the weight shift and often they begin to push off too late in the stride. Wasteful, tiring backslipping is the inevitable result.

Completing that weight shift sets the wax firmly in the snow; pushing off early holds that set and makes maximum use of the leg motion as well. Pay deliberate attention to both.

Pole Plant. As you reach forward and plant the pole, it should be leaning away from you at a slight angle. In this position (which varies from skier to skier, and from speed to speed) it *can be used immediately.* An efficient planting motion will merge smoothly into the push and follow-through.

Ski Pole Lock. Once planted in the snow, the pole will act like a lock. Continue to push as far back as you can—both for maximum drive, and also to prevent slipping. It's amazing the mileage one can get from the last half of the poling motion. *Work behind with your poles; work ahead with your skis.* Nowhere in touring is this axiom more apt.

Pole Release. As you near the end of your poling motion, relax your grip on the handle (the pole won't go anywhere

Pole release. As you near the end of your poling motion, be sure to relax your grip.

because of that strap around your hand). Grasping the pole tightly all the time will make a full follow-through physically impossible and is unnecessarily tiring. Concentrate on that follow-through; at the end of the motion you are loose, letting go, as if in your imagination, you'd flung that pole far away behind you.

Follow-through. An incomplete motion is a waste. At the end of the follow-through, the arm should be extended back as far back as it swings forward. Again, think in terms of the pendulum and don't be cramped or restrained. Now, by the way, you can see the reason for the exaggerated arm-swing exercises; flexibility in the shoulders is a must for a smooth follow-through.

A good, full followthrough in the diagonal stride. Note how far back the arm is extended.

Recovery. Just after the end of each follow-through, your arm and leg should have the opportunity to rest—recovering like pendulums from the exertion of the movement. Ideally, only half your body should be working at any one time; as you kick with one leg and pole with one arm, the other leg and arm should be recovering and resting.

Waste no motion. Bobbing, weaving, wobbling and swaying do not contribute to your forward motion. Avoid them. The same is true of your arms. Reach straight ahead and follow-through straight behind; don't let the arms slop out to the side or hook around your torso. If you've no instructor around to point out these unnecessary movements, you can sometimes spot them yourself by watching your shadow on the snow—if, of course, the angle of the sun is right.

All this may appear hideously complex on the printed page, but have faith; out on the snow it is not. Chances are you'll find many of these movements coming naturally; in fact, it may well be that you'll prefer to use this text only as an after-the-fact checklist—as the school child uses the answers in the back of his math book to verify an answer he already knows is right.

Diagonal Rest

After you get the diagonal down fairly well, try working on an interrupted variation, which is commonly used to rest the arms,

Diagonal rest. Rest the arms and the upper body as you glide along.

shoulders, and back. Often called the two-step diagonal, it works as follows. Get your standard diagonal rolling smoothly. Then start to inject, after every two diagonal strides, a couple of strides without planting the poles. Just swing them easily in the air, keeping the same rhythm, while gliding along on your skis. The basic cadence is: "pole, pole; glide, glide" ("pole" meaning *use your pole*; "glide" meaning do not).

Note that this diagonal rest technique can be viewed as an introduction to the various change-up techniques which will be covered later in this chapter.

Double-Poling

If the diagonal is the standard rhythmic workhorse of touring technique, then double-poling is the flamboyant flourish. In its place, it is the fastest technique, but it cannot be used everywhere; a long, gentle downhill slope is usually the ideal terrain

Double poling. Your arms, torso, and legs should all work together to propel you.

for double-poling. Another good situation for this technique is a fast or icy track.

Double-poling, too, is basically simple. Start out with a half-dozen or so diagonal strides until you're moving briskly along; then reach forward with both arms, plant the poles in unison, and push on through. As you reach forward with your arms, you should bring your upper body weight well out over the poles; then as your arms pole forcefully on through, let your torso bend ahead so that its leverage, and a simultaneous knee bend, will propel you along. The arm follow-through should be strong, like that of the diagonal. As you reach back, relax the hand grip and again pretend you're flinging those poles out behind you. Finally, recover for another go 'round by swinging your arms forward and raising your body to an upright position.

The key to efficient double-poling is arm and body power; you almost want to lunge into this one, then oomph on through. It's very dynamic and much fun.

Double poling, the followthrough. Pretend you're flinging those poles out behind you.

Double poling with kick. Note that the kick is completed before the poles are planted.

Double-Poling with Kick or Kicks

This is a combination technique that tosses one or more kicks between the basic double-poling thrusts. The purpose of adding these kicks is acceleration so that you'll have the necessary momentum as you start into the double-pole, which cannot be done from a standstill, or at slow speeds, without rapidly tiring the arms. The trick is to be sure to complete a kick before you begin the double-poling movement. This enables your arms and legs to help each other by counteraction, and your efficiency will increase sharply. The number of kicks you do depends on how much speed you want to build up before poling; it could be one, or just as easily five.

Many find this a harder technique to get into. Its demands on timing are somewhat greater than either the diagonal or double-poling alone; beginners often tend to get the kicks and the double-pole scrambled together. The best way out of this is a timed count; try it. Kick, double-pole; kick, double-pole. Or kick, kick, kick, double-pole. Say it aloud if it helps.

At the end of any double-pole you should be gliding briskly along. Take advantage of this by resting for an instant in that relaxed upright position before kicking (or double-poling) again.

Try working through these techniques and combinations—the diagonal, diagonal rest, double-poling, and double-poling with kicks—*individually* until you have learned each one well. This is the usual lesson format (perhaps a bit more detailed than some), and a good self-instruction sequence as well. However, don't belabor your learning process with endless drill on the practice track; you can work on your technique on an afternoon tour just as well.

Change Up

Only after you have each individual touring technique mastered should you work much on the change up; but do give it some time as you progress. A simple truth of almost any physical movement is this: if you repeat it over and over enough, chances are you'll tire, or even cramp. This is certainly true in touring, and one major reason you'll want to change up from one technique to another as you glide along. The other reasons for change up are snow condition, wax, and terrain.

There's no precise instruction involved here. Just work on making smooth, fluid transitions from one technique to another as the conditions require. Eventually, you should be able to shift from diagonal to double-poling, to diagonal rest, without the slightest hitch in your rhythm. Most skiers find this comes naturally with experience, but some deliberate polishing won't hurt.

Two more questions that are often asked:

• When should I use what technique? There's no pat answer to this one. By knowing them all and using them enough, you'll develop intuitive responses. The variables of ski touring—the snow, the track (if you're on one), the terrain, the wax, and (most important of all) your own condition—will determine where you come out, and when you change up from one technique to another. The point is to master them individually and then to be able to shift smoothly and at will from any one to any other. Like the proverbial chain, your technique is only as strong as its weakest link.

• Do I need to know all these techniques? Certainly not. Many people who have been touring for years don't. The point, however, is that the description of basic touring techniques you've just read has exhausted the subject. There are no more! With this limited number of options open to you, why not learn them all? Be able to use each one when you feel the need, and change up from one to another. It's a matter of being versatile, flexible and loose.

TECHNIQUE: A FEW POINTERS

As you're developing and refining your touring technique, keep the following suggestions in mind. They could carry you a long way and eliminate some confusion.

• *Except for lying down and sitting, standing straight up is the most relaxing position for your body. Why not ski that way whenever possible?*

• *Don't bend your knees any more than the conditions require. It's bound to be tiring and that's not what touring is about.*

• *Physical conditioning will not give you speed, but technique will. Good technique will often make up for poor conditioning.*

• *The skier who works the hardest does not necessarily ski the fastest or travel the greatest distance. If his technique is weak, he will only be working hard.*

• *When your skis slip back or stick in the snow, don't be quick to blame the wax, for chances are your problem is technique. Waxing and technique go hand in hand. Good technique will make your wax work.*

• *Don't depend on your poles for balance; their purpose is propulsion.*

Stationary Turns

Put a three- or four-year-old child on touring skis, send him away from you, and then ask him to turn around. Chances are he'll do it without blinking simply by moving his skis, little by little, in a gradual arc until he's facing you. This is the essence of the basic level ground turn. We adults have since systematized and defined this activity—and in one case given it a

Step turn around the tips of the skis. The tracks in the snow tell the story here. The turn around the tails of the skis simply reverses this maneuver.

special refinement that makes it possible to turn on a dime and on a 45-degree slope. Here's the run-down on these stationary turns.

Step Turn Around Tails. Keep the tails of your skis a few inches apart, and move or lift one tip away from the other until the skis form a "V" with those tails at its base. Then move the ski that's away from the direction you want to turn parallel to the other. As you step from one ski to another, there will be a complete weight shift; otherwise you'll not be able to lift the ski you want to move. Repeat the process five or so times until you're turned around.

Step Turn Around Tips. In this turn, the tips of the skis, instead of the tails, form the base of an inverted "V" (or the top of an "A"); otherwise it's the same as the previous turn.

Step Turn Around Tips and Tails. This turn is a combination of the first two, as the name implies. Start out with that "V" at the tail of the skis; then let it go to the tips, and so forth—so that, in effect, you are pivoting around the middle of the ski.

The kick turn. It looks much more awkward than it really is.

This combination turn is a little quicker than either one. You'll naturally fall into it after you master these simple turns.

Kick Turn. This is the quickest and most efficient stationary turn of all; it's useful anywhere from the flat to the slope of a genuinely steep hill. However, until you get used to the kick turn, it can create slight leg twisting that can feel rather awkward.

Start with a turn to the right. The first key is planting the poles to insure your balance. With the skis in a normal parallel position, set your left pole slightly beyond, and to the left of, the tip of that ski; then set the right pole slightly behind and to the right of the tail of that ski. At this point you'll be pivoted and facing to the right. Be sure you're good and stable before proceeding.

Now for the turn. Keeping your poles in place, kick the right ski up until it's standing vertically with its tail sitting in the snow. Check your steadiness at this point to be sure it's still with you. Then let the tip of that right ski swing out and around (gravity will largely take care of this) until it is parallel with the other, but facing in the *opposite* direction. The first few times you do this, it will seem a position of considerable perplexity, but getting out of it is easy. Just lift the left ski, and swing it around alongside the right, and the turn is complete.

The kick turn is a thing of infinite variations all based on the same principle. You can experiment and pick these up as you go along.

Moving Turns

The three step turns can also be done with great ease and efficiency when you're on the move and want to change direc-

The skating turn. Push off with the outside ski as you wheel around the corner.

tion. In fact, if any turns are universal for the tour skier, these maneuvers are. They are applicable not only on the flat, but also when you're traveling either up or downhill. You can and should be able to do any of these turns while skiing the diagonal, or double-poling, without breaking your rhythm at all.

Skating Turn (Around Tails). If you've ever ice or roller skated at all, this maneuver will be self-evident; the name is both descriptive and accurate.

Take the turn to the left. As you enter it bend your knees, pick up the left (or inside) ski and point it a few degrees to the left. Then push off firmly (or skate) with your right ski, unweight it, and bring it in line with the left one. Three or four quick skating strides like this will get you around a 90-degree turn. Be sure to bend the knees and crouch low to maintain your balance as you wheel around the turn.

Note that the skating turn increases your speed, a result of the pushing off motion that propels you around those bends and corners in the trail.

Moving turn around the tips of the skis. This time, point the outside ski in a few degrees as you come around the corner.

Turn Around Tips. Here's one that will slow you down if you are skiing downhill. Try it to the left. As you enter the turn, again drop into a noticeable crouch, but this time pick up the *right* (or outside) ski, point it a few degrees inward, transfer your weight to it and then bring the left ski alongside. As with the skating turn, three or four quick strides will take you through a 90-degree turn. The lack of a push off, and the slight stemming (or breaking) effect of the ski, are what help slow you down.

On the flat, one can maintain or even increase his speed through the turn by driving the pointed ski forward.

Combination Turn Around Tips and Tails. This is the moving turn you'll probably fall into naturally after you've worked on the first two. Your first step through the turn will be the ice skating maneuver; your second will change to around the tip, and so forth. This combination will enable you to cut sharper corners than either of the first two turns alone.

Falling, Getting Up

Every now and again you'll fall, which is normal enough. If you feel yourself going down (in touring, you frequently have time), try to land on your side, or on your seat, avoiding various forms of forward dives or plunges. In touring, beginners usually consider the fall a safe and useful method of stopping.

Getting up in soft snow can sometimes be a chore; push down normally with your arm and it will only sink in deeper. So let your poles come to the rescue. The most common method is to remove the straps from your wrists, grip the poles together (one hand near the baskets, the other near the handles), plant the tips in the snow and push yourself back up. If the snow is too soft for that, then lay the poles down in an "X" and push up from the point where they cross; the poles will act like a snowshoe and give you the support you need. A third approach is simply to drop the poles, wriggle around until you're kneeling on your skis; then push yourself up.

On the flat, you can have your skis pointed in any direction when getting up and have no problems. On the hill, however, be sure your skis are horizontal (at a right angle with the slope of the hill, pointing neither up or down) so that you won't slip and flop back in the snow when half way up.

TECHNIQUE: ON THE HILL

Now move to those beckoning slopes—some steep, others gradual. These require special techniques of their own, be it for climbing or for downhill running. Like many other elements of the sport, one can manage decently enough without mastery of all these maneuvers. Again, since so little of this is complex or demanding, and since it all makes life easier and more fun out in the snow, why not?

With good technique and the proper wax, you can walk straight up many hills.

If the hill is too steep, just angle up in a long, easy traverse.

Climbing

Going up a hill can be a most troublesome and tiring experience for anyone who doesn't know how to handle it. Backslipping, in particular, drains one's energies very quickly; the effect can be like that of an endless treadmill. However, such an ordeal can be readily avoided.

First of all, here's where waxing for firm grip pays special dividends. Though no substitute for sound technique, waxing certainly goes hand in hand with it. Chances are that you'll be amazed the first time you take off and actually discover yourself skiing uphill. Many who have done both feel it's easier than hiking or backpacking.

Traverse. The first rule of climbing on skis is: don't tackle *any* hill at a pitch so steep that you'll risk slipping back, tensing up to prevent it (this is often overlooked and very important; even if you don't slip an inch, you can still wear yourself thin fighting it) or depending on your poles to keep you in place. In

If you want to work up the hill a bit more quickly, combine some side-stepping with the normal traverse. Take one glide forward, then one step up—all the way.

fact, you should use your poles less on longer climbs than you do on the flat. Much better to move up a hill in a series of gradual zig-zag traverses, each one at a reasonable, non-slip angle across the slope. A kick turn will take care of changes in direction at the end of each traverse (do make sure your skis are on the level before making those turns). Hill climbing on skis should be an easy, relaxed experience, not an exhausting chore.

Traverse with Steps. A variation of the usual traverse, which allows you to gain altitude more quickly with little added exertion, is simply to take an uphill side-step with the upper ski for every stride forward with the lower ski. The actual pitch of the ski going up the hill is no greater, but you reach the top more quickly.

Herringbone and Half-Herringbone. Except in very deep snow, the half- and full-herringbone are useful techniques if you want to head straight up a steep hill. Stride normally up as long as you can without tensing, then let your skis separate into a "V" with the tails forming its base. Step firmly forward first with one ski, then the other, completing the weight shift each

The half-herringbone and the herringbone. Here the tracks tell the story.

time. The tracks you leave behind in the snow will resemble the pattern of an oversize herringbone. The half-herringbone comes in when you want to traverse uphill at a steeper angle than normally possible. Here you make a half-"V" with the lower ski, keeping the upper ski pointing in the direction you are going. In both herringbones, finish each step by shifting the weight fully and *straightening* that weighted leg. The latter movement will not only give your ski a firmer grip, it will also put you briefly in that relaxed, upright resting position, and ease your climb.

If the snow condition makes it necessary, you can accentuate the grip of the herringboned ski (one or both) by pushing the inside edge into the snow with an inward thrust of the knee. If snow is icy or handpacked, you'll have to do this; if your skis are sinking in a few inches or more, you won't.

A few important pointers for all uphill climbing:

• Don't lean forward any more than you would on the flat; bending ahead only increases your chances of slipping back. Try to climb with your body almost at a right angle to the slope; with this direction of pressure, your wax will hold more effectively.

• Plant your poles firmly in the snow so they can be locked in case you feel yourself beginning to slip back. Keeping a little weight on the pole strap as you follow through will maintain the lock position.

• Remember that axiom, "Work ahead with the skis; work behind with the poles." This is applicable to all methods of climbing: the traverses, the straight uphill stride, the half-herringbone and the herringbone.

• In whatever way you're attacking the slope, be sure to complete your weight shift with every stride or herringbone step. A firmly weighted ski is a solid ski; it stands much less a chance of slipping back.

Downhill

If you have done much alpine skiing, you've a pretty fair head start here. If you haven't, downhilling is something special for the tour skier to master, for it can be a rare delight—especially in areas of the United States and Canada where one can get into the mountains and to that wondrous, wide open country above the timberline. A ski climb to a summit or some similar high point, followed by a long, leisurely run down from the summit, can be one of those ultimate experiences that one associates with those romantic, creative ski movies. Doing this is not such a remote possibility. For many tour skiers in the Rockies and Sierras, for example, it is a regular weekend event.

An easy downhill run—normal position.

Basic Downhill Running. On touring skis this is about the same as it is on the alpine models. The skis are parallel, and six or so inches apart; the body straight but not stiff; the knees slightly flexed for balance; the arms at the side and bent easily at the elbows; hands hip-high, forward and slightly out from the body; poles pointing back at about a 45-degree angle. Though some cross-country racers have been clocked at over 40 mph on downslopes, sheer speed is not usually what touring is all about. If you must, you can barrel downhill on touring skis in the basic position. Most people, however, prefer more gradual downward traverses back and forth over the slope. At faster speeds, you'll find yourself naturally bending your knees more, both for balance and to absorb the shock from bumps and other variations on the terrain. At lower speeds, you can stand almost straight in the energy-saving, relaxed upright position.

Telemark Position. For the downhill run, the above is standard. The only deviation is the classic Telemark position that orginated in the Norwegian province of the same name in the nineteenth century. It's tricky until you get the hang of it (mostly a matter of balance), and also exquisitely graceful. For the normal, full Telemark position, simply slide one ski ahead of the other until binding and ski tip are more or less even. Both

For added stability, for-
ward and back, dip into
the Telemark position.

knees will drop into a pronounced bend, but keep your upper
body straight—no bending at the waist. Weight should be
evenly distributed over both skis (beginners often tend to hold
it too far back); arms and poles are carried conveniently out to
the side for balance.

The Telemark position will give you added stability, forward and back. It is especially useful when your downhill run
takes you across a snow-covered ditch, over bumps, or through
varying fast and slow snow conditions. Note too, that this
position has infinite variations. Traveling over slight bumps
and dips, you often won't need the full Telemark; you can
get all the balance you need simply by advancing one ski a
foot or so ahead of the other. In some cases, too, you'll want to
shift most of your weight to the back ski so you won't pitch
forward (as, for example, when you're running from fast snow
into slow) or to the front one (vice versa). Don't think of the
Telemark as a fixed position; be ready to vary it according to
snow conditions, and terrain.

Checking and Stopping

On many downhill runs there comes that agonizing moment when a tree, boulder, hole or creek looms in front of you. Or perhaps, you suddenly realize that you're traveling too fast, and would simply like to slow down, so you can maneuver more sharply. Two basic methods will take care of you under these circumstances.

Checking with poles. Flick the tips of your poles into the snow to slow down.

Checking and stopping. (Above right) the half snowplow. (Left and right) the snowplow combined with checking with poles and the full snowplow.

Checking with Poles. While continuing to ski straight, simply bring your elbows in, lay your forearms out, and flick the tips of both poles together into the snow slightly ahead of you. Again and again and again. Try to absorb most of the shock from this pole-braking with your shoulders. Don't try to stop yourself this way; just keep your speed in check—maybe down to about half. Checking with poles can be particularly useful when you're traveling through a dense woods or in a deep track, and have no room to maneuver with your skis.

Snowplow and Half-Snowplow. That well-tested warhorse of the beginning alpine skiers, the snowplow, is also an old standby for those who tour. Bend your knees slightly (while keeping the upper body straight), put pressure on the inside edges of your skis as needed, keep the tips close together, and let the tails ease outward until you're sliding downhill in a steady, controlled "V". The knee and edge pressure are critical; they cause the ski to bite into the snow and supply the main braking power. You can coast slowly in the snowplow position by bending your knees and edging moderately; you can come to a full stop by doing both more emphatically.

A common variation often used by tour skiers is the half-snowplow. Here only one ski moves into the braking snowplow position while the other stays in the track, or points straight downhill. This can be tiring on the snowplowing leg; it's smart to switch over to the other and then alternate back if you do this for any extended distance.

Combination Snowplow and Checking with Poles. This is just exactly what the name implies. Used together, these two techniques are sometimes handy, particularly when neither one alone is sufficient to check you.

Turning

The tour skier's turns also borrow heavily from those of his alpine counterpart. In fact, when the snow conditions are right, it's all but impossible to distinguish an accomplished tour skier from the downhiller, for both can maneuver in identical style.

For most of today's recreational tour skiers, three basic turns will more than suffice.

A snowplow turn to the right.

Snowplow Turn. Start from the straight snowplow position. For a turn to the right, gradually transfer more of your weight to the left ski, which will then become the outside ski of the turn. This can be done at low speeds under complete control.

Stem Turn. Start this turn from a downhill traverse in the relaxed, upright position. Slowly stem (or "V") out the tail of the uphill ski, and then ease your weight onto that stemmed ski; then sideslip and return to the traverse position. The upper body should be angled over the weighted ski and the outside shoulder drawn slightly back. This combination of movements will bring you smoothly through the turn.

Stem Christie. Again start from a gradual downhill traverse in that relaxed upright position. This time do a slight sinking motion as you stem the uphill ski. Then with an up-forward movement, transfer your weight to the stemmed, outside ski and bring the inside ski parallel with it; this will take you half-way through the turn. To complete the turn, do a second sinking motion, combined with a slight rotation of the hips and shoulders in the opposite direction of the turn. As you swing fully around, you'll want to rise again to the normal traverse position.

Telemark Turn. This is not a basic turn, but it is one of the sweetest maneuvers of the sport and, for that reason alone, deserves comment. The Telemark turn is also the exclusive property of the touring fraternity. With his heel locked to the ski, the alpine enthusiast hasn't the necessary freedom of movement to execute it.

Here's how. Once again start out in a gentle downhill traverse, and then fall forward into the Telemark position with the uphill ski advanced. As you do this, simultaneously weight and point that leading ski inward—in the direction of your turn. You may also want to edge it a bit for surer steering. The combination of these efforts will send you into a smooth, arc-like turn; when you're done, simply bring your skis back together again.

Telemark turn to the left.

The Telemark turn works beautifully in powder snow and can be done at quite slow speeds. The key here is balance, not strength or force; carry your arms conveniently out to the side for stability. If you're prone to wobbling, perfecting this turn will take some concentrated practice. You may decide to pass on it all together. This is by no means an essential maneuver; it is, however, an act of ballet-like grace in which many find astonishing pleasure. Link together a series of smooth Telemark turns on a long, gentle slope and you may well discover sensations experienced in pure dance.

Other Turns. This by no means exhausts the variety of downhill turns possible for the tour skier. The entire range of advanced alpine maneuvers—christie, parallel, short swing, wedel, etc.—are all possible if done from the heels with one's weight over the center or well back on the skis. This means they are just as possible with touring equipment as they are with downhill gear.

The tour skier knows only two limits on his freedom to execute and enjoy turns. First is snow condition. You're restricted pretty much to the softer snow unless your skis have steel edges; if they do, then it's possible for you to handle even

A parallel turn on touring skis? Get your technique together and it's no problem at all—as long as the snow conditions are right.

ice. Second, since you don't rely on the added support of heavy alpine equipment (especially boots and bindings), your technique must be finer; for example, you must learn to carry your weight back on the skis yourself, rather than having it more or less anchored there for you.

In other words, it's perfectly possible for an able skier with touring equipment to hop an alpine chairlift or gondola, ride to the top of the mountain, and ski down just about as he pleases. The skinny skis, lightweight boots, and simple bindings might just raise a few eyebrows. Perhaps someday touring equipment will actually revolutionize the downhill sport. The possibility might not be that remote, once people discover they can have just as much fun without lugging around all that heavy alpine gear.

TERRAIN UTILIZATION

The more you wander about on touring skis, the more you should find yourself using every bump and dip in the terrain to your advantage. The skilled racer must do this often and intuitively to gain precious seconds along the course; he must also hone this ability with tough, intense concentration. The recreational skier can achieve all the proficiency he needs more gradually and with much less attention. He has no more at stake than the loss of an easier, more relaxed tour.

Good terrain utilization involves myriad little maneuvers, almost all designed to take advantage of gravity and turns. At the foot of a gentle hill, pushing off with poles or ski can give you an extra yard or two of glide, and probably save you a stride. Doing the same thing as you start down a dip in the track will take you more easily up the far side. If there's an uneven pitch in the trail—say a spot where the right ski must travel over a slight bump, while the left stays on the flat—don't bother to work over that bump. Let your weight shift toward the left until the right ski rides lightly over the obstacle; then push off with the latter on the downward side.

Terrain utilization. Artificially made "bicycle bumps" are good for practicing. Note how the left ski is working on the downhill side of one bump, while the right ski is beginning to move easily up the next.

Make yourself conscious of these small efforts as you get into touring, but don't belabor them. Casual practice and application will lead to a tour skier's "sixth sense" that will save you progressively more effort.

5

Waxing

Waxing may be the ultimate bogeyman of ski touring. No other aspect of the sport is the subject of more confusing or conflicting advice. On any given morning, with any given group, you will find confirmed waxers, confirmed anti-waxers, and all shades of opinion in between. Some will swear by blue wax, some by green, one or two by light green, and a couple more by whatever happens to be on their skis. In a few hours, either all will forget about it, or all but the last will find reason to change or rewax. Waxing debate is part of the touring mystique and has been for years; in this sport of simplicity, some psychological need has demanded that somewhere there be a counterbalance of complexity. Waxing is it.

Yet for the tour skier, waxing is, in truth, reasonably simple.

The basic point is to get something on the bottoms of your skis that will allow them to slide or grip when you want them to. In principle it works like this.

Grip. Fresh snow has many sharp edges. Some kinds of snow are crystalline, each flake a tiny hexagon with myriad delicate points and spikes; other forms include minute plates, columns, prisms, needles, and irregular particles. After a few days of sun or warm weather, or just sitting, any snow tends to deteriorate a bit, but under the microscope, it is still very rough. Touring wax takes advantage of this property. Wax is softer than snow, and the thousands of minute points and edges jab into it, causing the ski to grip or hold. This interaction allows one to ski uphill, a feat that seldom fails to delight and amaze the beginning tourer.

Glide. Break the grip and begin to move the ski, and something else happens: friction between wax and snow builds heat, which creates a thin film of water between the two. This film acts as a lubricant and away you glide.

Temperature, the condition of the snow (is it fresh or old?), and its moisture content are the three variables that control wax performance and dictate wax selection. The point is to match the wax with snow condition: a hard wax for cold, brittle snow; a softer wax for warmer, mushier snow. The goal is to get the proper balance between grip and glide.

For the racer, this can be both a wicked chore and an exacting skill. The balance he must achieve is very delicate; he wants both maximum glide and dependable grip. However, for the tour skier waxing is far less critical; his concern is to avoid the extremes of inconvenience. He does not want to slip going up hills; neither does he care to have the snow stick to his skis and ball up while he is cruising along the flat or coasting downhill. Both can be exhausting, but the middle ground between these extremes is broad and the excess of work easily avoided. As long as the tour skier has a good hold going uphill, and a reasonable glide coming down, he will be happy. That combination is not that difficult to achieve.

KINDS OF SNOW

The person who hasn't thought about it is usually amazed to discover how structurally varied snow can be. The tour skier doesn't need to worry about these complexities unless he happens to be interested; he has two concerns: moisture content and basic type.

Moisture content has a direct bearing on the thin film of water that builds between wax and snow when the ski is moving. With a wet snow, that film forms more quickly, and the ski slides more readily; waxing for grip becomes a prime consideration. With drier snow, something approaching the converse becomes true. Determining this moisture content is a fairly simple matter; the following guidelines will do the job.

• If the air temperature is below 32 degrees F., all snow tends to be dry.

• Above 32 degrees (freezing), pick the snow up with your hands. If you can make a snowball, then it's wet; if you can't, it's dry. Mischievous childhood experience and wisdom are useful to recall in assessing moisture content.

Snow types are a hair more subtle, but no more. Think of them in three basic categories, all related to those crystalline structures that jab into the wax:

Corking smooth a layer of hard running wax.

• Fresh, fine snow with many sharp, gripping points and edges is loose and puffy.

• Coarse snow develops after fresh snow has set for several days; even if it remains cold, evaporation will begin to blunt those points and edges.

• Granular "corn" snow (the term must come from some imaginative chap who dreamed he was skiing upon great mounds of kernels) has melted and refrozen, often several times. Now the points and edges are becoming almost dull.

The relation of these snow types to wax is self-evident: the greater the natural jabbing and penetrating ability of the snow, the harder the wax (otherwise you won't glide at all); as those gripping qualities decrease, the wax should be appropriately softer.

KINDS OF WAXES

Walk into a well-stocked touring shop and you're liable to be confronted with a tier of shelves or a counter loaded with a formidable array of waxes packaged in brightly colored tins and tubes. At least a dozen manufacturers (almost all European) are now marketing waxes in the United States. American manufacturers are sure to get into the business as the sport continues to grow.

Currently available lines include from three to thirteen different kinds of wax—but the complexity is much less than it first seems. To begin with, there are only three kinds of waxes: base waxes (these are primarily for protecting the bottom of the ski), binders, and running waxes (these are what actually ride over the snow).

Base Wax

For most tour skiers, base wax (or as the Swedes call it, *grundvalla*) means one thing: pine tar. True, there have been some other base waxes around, but over the years pine tar and pine tar compounds have more than covered the field. They do their job well; people are used to them; and they have been around long enough to become part of the basic mystique of touring.

As long as the wood ski with the birch or hickory bottom stays with us, pine tar will do likewise. This means its future is now limited, but the end still remains a ways down the road. For the time being then, this base wax serves two important purposes:

• It impregnates and seals the wood sole of the ski and keeps it from getting wet. Constant soaking and drying is not good for any wood and can sometimes cause warping; in addition, a waterlogged ski is a heavy ski and more to be lugged around.

• It holds the running waxes better than bare wood. If that bare wood is wet, it will not take the running waxes at all.

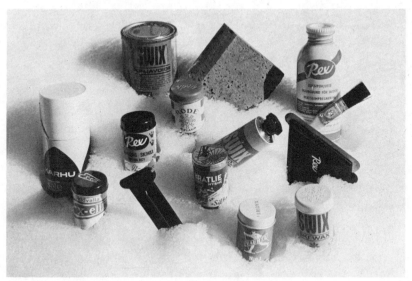

An assortment of waxes, plus cork and scrapers.

Pine tar also makes a decent running wax in its own right, especially in colder, new snow conditions.

The traditional way of applying pine tar is with brush, torch, and rag. First paint on a thin layer; then heat it with the torch (usually butane with a fan nozzle) until it just begins to bubble. As this happens, you'll notice that the tar is also absorbed into the wood. Continue to brush on more until the ski stops taking it (to get maximum impregnation *and* protection). Keeping the ski wet in this way also prevents it from burning. Finally, rub the ski down with a rag, being sure to remove all the excess. When you're done, the bottom should be a smooth, even brown, as the ski gets older and is retarred five or six times, that color will darken noticeably.

A few words of caution:
• Some new skis come through with a protective coating; this must be removed before the initial tarring or you won't get any penetration. Scrape or use fine sandpaper as necessary.
• On subsequent tarrings, preparation is unnecessary. If there's running wax on the bottom, simply burn it in.
• Work the whole ski at once with a long, even stroke; do your best to keep an even temperature from tip to tail (to avoid possible warping).
• Do not char the ski; always keep the torch moving and not too close to the bottom; err on the side of caution.

Pine tarring has a reputation for being messy, but except perhaps for the first time you try it, this need not be so. The person who's done it a few times should find it a simple, clean, five-minute task; an experienced hand wouldn't hesitate to pine tar a ski while wearing his tuxedo.

This method unquestionably impregnates and seals the ski better than any other. Also, the rich, pungent aroma of pine tar is part of the romance of touring. However, other alternatives are available. Base wax now also comes in a paint-on, air drying formula and in aerosol spray cans. In neither case is a torch necessary, but the skis should be given ample time to dry (this varies with different brands, so check instructions on the can). These methods do not seal the ski as well as heating. The third choice is to have a ski shop burn in the pine tar for you; this usually costs about a dollar, though many places do it free on a new pair of skis.

Final note: pine tar is really more a preparation than anything else. Unless you ski constantly, or in conditions that are especially rough on your skis, application is a twice-a-year proposition, three times at the most.

Binders

These are actually a kind of base wax (and in fact are sometimes labeled as such). They come as a sticky hard wax that must be either crayoned onto the ski and rubbed smooth with a cork, or melted lightly with a torch and scraped smooth. Binders are sometimes used between the pine tar and the running wax—sometimes in place of the pine tar itself. As the name implies, this wax helps bind the running wax to whatever is beneath it; it also adds some pine tar-type protection. For the most part, binders are a refinement, used almost exclusively by racers who need to count on a waxing that will not wear off. If you're a recreational skier using wood-bottom skis, don't bother with this wax unless you enjoy complications.

However, if your skis have the new synthetic bottoms, it may pay to give the binder a second look. The less perfect of these skis do not always hold running waxes as well as they might; since they cannot be pine-tarred, the binder can come in handy.

This is surely a temporary situation. With today's better synthetic bottoms, binders are wholly unnecessary. The cellulose fiber-epoxy resin formula now used on the Finnish Karhu skis holds running waxes beautifully because of the wood-like quality of those tiny fibers. As other manufacturers improve their bottoms—and they most certainly will—the binder wax will once again revert to the exclusive realm of the racer.

Running Waxes

Here's where the apparent complexity sets in, where the debate becomes thick, and the mystique a muddle or a joy depending on your point of view. First of all, a definition: running waxes are what ride directly over the snow. There are two forms:

Hard waxes come in small tins and are crayoned on, then rubbed smooth with a cork; the ski must be dry when these are applied. The harder waxes act and feel more or less like candle wax (even though they're petroleum-based synthetics); the softer ones are quite tacky. Generally speaking, these waxes are for new snow and colder temperatures.

Klisters are of thick liquid consistency, usually available in tubes; a new packaging is more like a shaving cream can. In Swedish, *klister* means "glue"; the name is most deserved, since these waxes are downright gooey. They are squeezed on in squiggles, then smoothed with a metal or plastic scraper (the heel of your hand will do just as well); again your skis should be dry. It is not necessary to put klisters in the groove of the ski. Generally speaking they are for icy conditions, or very wet snow.

The standard line of running waxes consists of six hard and four klisters. Both containers and the waxes themselves are coded more or less according to the color spectrum: cool colors for colder snow conditions; warmer colors for above freezing conditions. At least this is approximate and standard. However, some maverick lines have their own color schemes with golds, silvers, and whatnot.

Manufacturers do two things to unravel this situation. The usual snow condition for each wax is printed, sometimes in Pidgin English only, on the can or tube: "For new fallen snow by thaw and slop weather," is the specification on Rex yellow. Also, each manufacturer publishes a chart for its waxes that specifies use. None of these is infallible (snow conditions are too variable, subtle, and fickle for that), but all are generally reliable and will get you into the ballpark.

THE MYSTERIES OF WAXING UNRAVELED

Every major max manufacturer has developed a chart to codify and clarify the use of its products.This chart, prepared for the Finnish Rex waxes, is as lucid and precise as you'll find. When you're dealing with up to six hard running waxes and four klisters, something like this is handy to have—even though many experienced tour skiers will insist you rarely have any business carrying more than three or four different kinds of wax at a time.

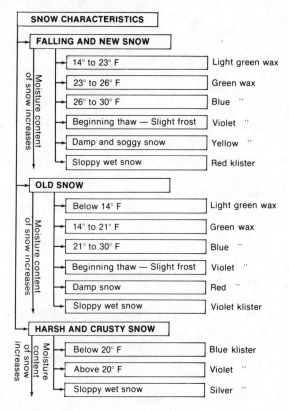

SNOW CHARACTERISTICS		
FALLING AND NEW SNOW		
	14° to 23° F	Light green wax
	23° to 26° F	Green wax
	26° to 30° F	Blue "
	Beginning thaw — Slight frost	Violet "
	Damp and soggy snow	Yellow "
	Sloppy wet snow	Red klister
OLD SNOW		
	Below 14° F	Light green wax
	14° to 21° F	Green wax
	21° to 30° F	Blue "
	Beginning thaw — Slight frost	Violet "
	Damp snow	Red "
	Sloppy wet snow	Violet klister
HARSH AND CRUSTY SNOW		
	Below 20° F	Blue klister
	Above 20° F	Violet "
	Sloppy wet snow	Silver "

(Moisture content of snow increases)

Brands

It's best to start out with one brand of wax and stick with it for a spell. Get used to its particular properties so you know what it will and won't do. Swix, Rex, and Rode are the three most commonly marketed brand names in the United States; they're usually handy when your stock runs out. This doesn't make them any better or worse than the others—just available, which can be important. If another brand is more readily available where you live and ski, use it.

HOW TO WAX

It is easy to ramble on at heady length about this; however, the following is really all that needs to be said.

• Keep waxing simple. Swix and Rex, for example, both market beginner's packs that contain only three hard waxes. These cover the spectrum reasonably enough for anyone just getting into the sport. Many experienced skiers still carry only three or four waxes, plus a klister in the spring.

• Waxing at home or in the garage before the tour is largely guesswork, also a waste of time. Unless you know the conditions where you will ski, wait. The sensible approach is to drive where you're going, get out of the car and ski for five or ten minutes on whatever wax you have on your skis (unless there's a glaring need to change). When you stop for your first rest, or to peel off a layer of clothing, you'll know if you've been slipping or sticking and can now wax accordingly. Trial and error is a wise teacher; in touring she's gentle as well.

• Waxes vary in consistency; some are hard while others are soft. This has an important practical consequence: you can rub a soft wax over a hard one, but not easily vice versa. Thus, if you absolutely must wax before leaving home and don't know the conditions of the area you plan to ski, put on a cool, hard wax—probably either green or blue. You can always run a soft one over it later; on the other hand, scraping off a soft wax can be a chore.

• For the tour skier a thermometer is largely academic. Feeling the skis actually grip and glide on the snow will tell you all you need to know, and more precisely than any thermometer. Take one if you wish, as a guide (special outdoor models, cased for protection, are available in reasonably stocked touring shops). By the way, the jury is still out on whether to hold the thermometer in the air or stick it in the snow. Swix says: "Begin by reading the air temperature." Rex says: "The best thing to do is measure the temperature of the snow itself." Experiment with both to determine your preference. Air temperature is usually a sufficient indicator, and remember that snow can never be warmer than 32 degrees F. (if it is, then it shouldn't be snow).

• Many people overdo their waxing (again part of the mystique). Unless you enjoy it for its own sake, wax only when you need to (which is when your skis are moving poorly). In the Rockies, it's commonplace for one wax to do the job for an entire week or more; the snow is consistently light and dry, and easy on a coat of wax. In New England—where snow is often wet and abrasive, where morning and afternoon may be as different as January and May—one must adapt and rewax accordingly.

• If your glide is good, but you have trouble going uphill, first add a heavier coating of the wax you have on; thicker layers of any wax give more grip. If that doesn't turn the trick, try applying what is called a "kicker." Go to the next warmest wax you have and rub it in for a couple of feet on the middle of the ski under your boot. This will improve your grip, with little or

Chances are you could find four or five different kinds of wax in use here, and they're all working well enough.

no effect on your glide. As the temperature drops late in the day, you may have to remove your kicker; scraping off two feet of wax is much easier than cleaning the entire ski (a fringe benefit from this kind of waxing). Often, however, the kicker will wear off of its own accord, and you won't have to give it a second thought.

• In areas where sticky snow is common, some people carry a stick of plain, everyday store paraffin. It is a fast wax, but it wears off very quickly, usually in a half mile. When the snow is clinging to your skis, and no wax will keep it off, paraffin will often come to the rescue. Many tour skiers think of paraffin as "a good wax to help you home" on those variable days when the snow suddenly and unexpectedly turns sticky.

• Usually a skier waxes to fit the snow, but there can be times when it's more sensible for him to find the snow that fits his wax. This is especially so on those rare, frustrating days when the snow condition seems to change every 50 yards. On open meadows it is wet; on south-facing slopes it is wetter; on north-facing slopes it is dry and powdery; in the woods it is something else. Stopping repeatedly to rewax isn't the answer. A more plausible solution is to ski as much as possible on snow that fits your wax; stay in the open, or in the woods as the case may be. Just do the best possible across those bad spots, which route adjustment should keep to a minimum.

If you still have trouble, two causes are possible. First, you may have encountered a snow condition for which there is simply no wax made (a combination of freshly fallen wet snow, warm weather, and trail breaking is next to impossible). This happens rarely, but when it does, your best bet is not to ski. Second, your technique may need work, for there is no wax made that fits a tour skier who cannot glide or climb properly. Many is the skier who waxes and rewaxes in an effort to stop his skis from backslipping or sticking on the snow, when all along his problem is imperfect technique. It never works. However, this is no consolation if you're out on a tour. Switch to a softer wax if your skis are slipping or to harder wax or paraffin if your skis are sticking, since these are the problems that are most tiring and most apt to spoil your day. These are not final solutions, but they'll get you home most easily.

6

The Day Tour

This is where the fun really begins.

You've had your lessons, done your spins around the practice track; bumps and ruffles in your technique are ironing themselves out nicely. Now you head for the hills.

Beginners almost inevitably get their first real taste of the sport on day tours, or often, half-day tours. The average tour covers from one to five miles, but on touring skis and with a grasp of the basics of technique this distance is far less than when you're afoot. Obviously you should start out with a group (be it three or twenty) that includes skiers more experienced than you. The route should be fairly gentle, and hopefully, scenic. If your eyes are open, it can't help but be interesting; after all, you'll be among friends in the midst of a winter you've probably never seen before.

The day tour is by no means limited to beginning skiers. Unless you gear up for an overnight stay in the snow, this is *the* tour. Most people tour for years, and many even a lifetime, without ever heading out for more than a day at a time. This simple fact is but one way of paying tribute to the pleasure, and

In Yosemite National Park, California.

infinite variety, of the touring sport; it does not require great amounts of time. No two days are the same, and neither are any two tours.

The good day tour doesn't just happen; planning and precaution are in order, even though you may venture no more than half a mile from the nearest paved road. The rest of this chapter will deal with the more serious aspects of the day tour. The fun is up to you.

Among the geysers, Yellowstone National Park, Wyoming.

Along Castle Creek at Ashcroft, Colorado.

WHAT TO CARRY

The purpose of any tour—be it for a few hours, a day or a week—is enjoyment. Conversely, you want to avoid unnecessary delays and discomfort. To insure this requires forethought. A broken ski or binding can mean a long, arduous walk back out. Similarly unpleasant consequences are true for sunburn, cold hands, wet feet, and even chapped lips.

Thus the first law of the tour skier's rucksack: *carry what you need to deal with anything that might go wrong.* On most tours, there'll be a few minor problems—perhaps a little sunburn or a broken pole basket. Since winter conditions can be severe, they greatly reduce one's margin of error. A lost summertime backpacker can hole up overnight and be little the worse for his experience; a lost tour skier can be in immediate trouble. An unexpected summer shower is unpleasant; in winter a sudden blizzard can pose real danger.

All in a day's pack. This collection will deal with all problems in five minutes or less.

Thus the obvious: *be prepared*; in fact, be a little over-prepared. Don't fool around with the odds; in the winter they can turn against you all too quickly.

Not every person will have to tote all the gear discussed in this section, but the tour leader must. Don't let that term, "tour leader," lull you into thinking what follows is for someone else. If you're touring alone (it can be a blissful experience, but is not usually advised), then you're the leader; if two people head out, one is the leader. Someone must be responsible.

(Note: If you're skiing around a lodge, or at a touring center where trails are well groomed and well patrolled, or enjoying a simple workout on a preplanned, short loop, all this gear and a rucksack are unnecessary. A spare ski tip in your hip pocket, some extra wax, and perhaps a small bag of hard candy—or whatever you prefer—will take care of you just fine.)

Now for the bag of tricks; this will take care of one person or twenty on an average day's tour (for overnight trips, see Chapter 7).

Repair Kit

Touring equipment is not supposed to break or come apart, but like every other manufactured product on this earth, it sometimes does. The exact array of repair gadgets you carry for these occasions is not as important as carrying what's necessary to get the job done. Furthermore, for enjoyment's sake, you should be able to do any repair job in no more than five minutes. Twenty minutes' fiddling with a broken binding in the cold snow can be unpleasant both for the repairman and those who are waiting for him. One final thought before beginning the list: keep this kit as light and compact as you can without sacrificing its usefulness. It will probably take time to get it together, so poke around the hardware store and test the gadgets. Some of those weird items that have always seemed utterly useless around the house may suddenly become just the thing. In addition to the items listed below, you'll also carry extra wax, cork, a scraper, and paraffin for rewaxing needs.

The following list comprises a representative repair kit.

• **Screwdriver and screws.** Occasionally a binding will pop a screw that is sure to vanish into the snow. One broken binding can ruin a tour; one screw can save it. It's best to carry a variety of fat, oversized screws that will bite firmly where a standard size has worked loose. Keep them in a small plastic sack so they don't scatter about. Also, a Phillips head screwdriver should be carried, in addition to the standard model.

• **Pliers.** These can fix everything from bindings to zippers. The locking Vise-Grip brand plier-wrench is hard to beat.

• **Extra binding parts.** Some people like to carry replacement parts for specific makes and models; this is fine if everyone along has the same binding, but that rarely happens. So carry items for general improvising; since any toe binding can be patched up with a *cable*, that's a must, as is some tough, light *baling wire*.

• **Tape.** As long as it's strong and sticks well under difficult conditions, the exact kind doesn't matter. Both athletic and friction tape are generally dependable. A split bamboo pole can be taped together very quickly; so can a rip in your pants.

• **Small drill.** If you must move a binding forward or back on the ski, you'll want a small drill to make new screw holes.

• **Small hammer.** Handy for a number of uses. One of those ingenious, compact combination tools — screwdriver + Phillips head + drill + pliers + hammer + awl + wire cutter—is an excellent item for the repair kit. Around the house, they're useless; out in the snow they can be a cure-all.

• **Safety pins.** The heavier ones are best; diaper pins are optional. Safety pins have fixed bindings and torn clothing, and have served well in many first-aid situations.

• **Spare ski tip.** A ski doesn't often break, but when one does, you're in trouble. It can happen when you're crossing a brook or ditch, when you take a spill coming downhill, or when you hit a snow-covered log or rock. Spare tips are made of aluminum or hard plastic. They clamp, screw or grip over the broken end of the ski and are surprisingly workable—far better than wading several miles through waist deep snow. Since the nearly indestructible metal and fiber glass skis are increasingly taking over from the wood, the spare tip seems destined for rare use. Even so, it's solid insurance—just in case.

The ingenious Norwegian-made Weswitco "tip-saw" includes a built-in saw for cutting firewood in an emergency; in addition, it also unfolds to be used as a combination scoop and shovel; finally, the saw cuts ice if you need to reach water, or use blocks of snow for making an igloo.

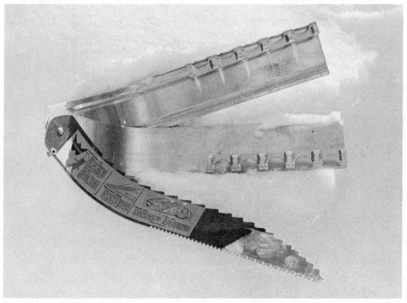

Supergadget: the Weswitco "Tipsaw" is spare ski tip, saw (wood and ice), and scoop all in one.

• **Spare pole strap.** A broken pole strap can hinder your technique; an extra can be taped on, or wound in place, with wire.

• **Spare pole basket.** Occasionally these come off and disappear into the snow. Being without a basket hampers poling, upsets balance and can therefore be surprisingly tiring.

• **Knife.** A simple, strong well-honed jackknife is fine. Some of the fancier models, especially the famous Swiss Army knives, include enough appendages to be small tool boxes in themselves.

That's the basic repair kit; vary it as you wish, as long as you're able to meet any situation that arises *in five minutes or less.* This is obviously a tour leader's collection; though sometimes others in the group carry an extra ski tip and a few other items.

Since the tour leader carries the responsibility for all who are with him, he will want to stock his pack with the following.

Clothing

Carry your own basic gear—usually extra pairs of socks and gloves, plus whatever layers of clothing you are not wearing. Everyone should always have clothing on hand for the coldest possible conditions (just in case the temperature plummets). Also bring along back-up socks and gloves in case one of the party is caught short.

Food

Bring your own lunch. This is always a matter of preference, but lean toward high-energy foods; think "hungry," since you'll be working up quite an appetite. You'll also want to carry a small drinking cup and a quart or so of water or other sensible drink (not alcohol); thirst, or dehydration, can strike deceptively and quickly in winter. For the rest, a few extras—a sand-

Lunch break along the trail.

wich, an orange, some candy bars or other high calorie snacks—should someone else need quick energy.

Saw and/or Stove

Since the traditional campfire has experienced increased disrepute (especially among conservationists who have rightly noted that, in many areas, trees have been stripped destructively bare for wood), consider heating that lunch-time soup and coffee (or tea) on one of the small backpack stoves. Don't use the butane models unless you know it's going to be fairly warm; at colder temperatures the stuff vaporizes poorly or not at all, meaning a negligible to nonexistent flame. The white gas stoves are much more reliable. For years the Swedish Svea-Optimus-Primus brands (all made by the same manufacturer and employing the same basic principle) have been standard; however, all the smaller models, such as the Svea 123 and the Optimus 8R, require priming, which in either wind or cold can be a tedious chore. Mountain Safety Research of Seattle has developed a similar lightweight design, the Model 9, which adds a small hand pump to eliminate priming and a flint "sparker" to do away with fussing with matches. These features, plus its high heat output, make it an excellent winter stove (it's reputed to melt snow at the rate of 20 quarts of water an hour!).

However, stoves are only stoves. If one of the party becomes chilled, a crackling campfire will be needed to warm him. Don't lug a heavy hatchet to chop wood. The backpack saws are lighter, safer, and more efficient. Among the best of these is the American-made folding Sven Saw. It weighs exactly a pound and can cut cordwood.

Topographic Map, Compass

The topographic maps published by the United States Geological Survey (USGS) are lovely, lucid, detailed, accurate, and the best outdoorsman's maps available. Contour lines indicate variations in terrain, and all significant landmarks and plant communities are designated. The 7½-minute series (just over 2½ inches to the mile, or to be exact, 1 inch for every 2,000 feet) is standard, with each sheet covering about 54 square miles. Though it has over 40,000 different maps in print, the USGS has still not yet charted every square inch of the United States; however, unless you're skiing in an unusually out-of-the-way area, you'll find one of these maps available. If you hit one of those "blank spots," chances are good that a less-detailed 15-minute USGS map (about one inch per mile) will cover it; Alaska, for example, is being done to this scale.

The 7½-minute maps cost 75¢ each; the 15-minute ones a dollar. These are carried by many backpacking and touring shops, or may be ordered directly from USGS regional offices or from national headquarters in Washington D.C. (for addresses, see Appendix B). Do not rely on maps published by the National Park Service, the United States Forest Service or the Bureau of Land Management. None are sufficiently detailed to tell you precisely where you are.

The Swedish Silva and Finnish Suunto compasses are excellent brands and widely available; both are designed for sportsmen, specially for use in map reading.

It should go without saying that the point of a map and compass is to enable you to find your way about whether you are in your own back yard or in completely new and foreign country. It is surprising how many people cannot do this (despite the fact that most of them think they can). The tour leader must be absolutely sure he can, even if he is traveling on a marked, packed trail; a good blizzard can obliterate all those familiar signs all too quickly.

Sunburn Lotion and Chapstick

Most beginners learn about the swift and searing effects of sun and snow the hard way; it's no fun at all. Carry ample supplies of lotion and chapstick and apply them liberally, especially in the spring.

Sunglasses

Snowblindness is comparatively rare, but even squinting all day can make for a mean headache. Everyone should carry his own sunglasses, but in case someone forgets, it's best for the leader to carry a spare pair. Goggles are generally useful only in strong winds, or when you're making a number of downhill runs. When a tour skier is gliding along at a normal pace, they often fog up. Special and expensive models have two-layer lenses, like thermopane glass, which effectively prevent this. If you prefer goggles, use them. Do not use downhill skiing goggles; on a tour skier, they usually *will* fog up.

First Aid Kit

The leader should carry a compact but adequate first-aid kit—even if he doesn't have cause to use it all winter long. Whether yours is from the corner drugstore or an outdoor specialty outfit, it should contain at least the following:

- **Standard band-aids**
- **Bandage compresses**
- **Plain square gauze pads**
- **Roll of gauze**
- **Larger triangular bandages**
- **Tourniquet**
- **Scissors**
- **Tweezers**
- **Aspirin**
- **Safety pins**
- **Disinfectant**

To this, be sure to add an Ace Bandage. It's designed for those rubber ankles and knees that act up or cave in unpredictably, and can serve a number of impromptu purposes as well.

The Mountaineer First Aid Kit is designed especially for backpackers, weighs less than a pound, and is widely distributed; incredibly, it contains 67 items. For $10.00, this is superb insurance.

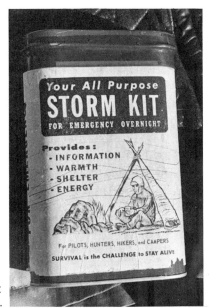

Emergency insurance in a 5¼ ×
3½ × 1½-inch tin.

Emergency Equipment

Chances of being forced into an overnight bivouac are slim, but the leader should be ready for it, able to keep all involved warm and well until dawn. Start with a flashlight; the little Mallory units are light and dependable. Add to that a good, compact emergency kit (the Mountain Rescue Council of Tacoma, Washington, packages an excellent one called the "Storm Kit"). If you decide to assemble your own, here is what you must have:

- **Matches** (individually waterproofed *and* in a waterproof container; dipping in hot paraffin will waterproof ordinary kitchen matches).
- **Candle** (for starting a fire)
- **Sugar** (for energy)
- **Salt** or **salt tablets** (to help overcome fatigue)
- **Bouillon cubes** (again, for energy)
- **Tea bags** (for a warm, penetrating drink)
- **Whistle** (for signalling; three blasts is the universal emergency call. A whistle carries better than the human voice; blowing one is much less exhausting than shouting.)
- **Signal mirror**
- **Space blanket** (primarily for warmth, also useful for signalling to aircraft)

The odds are well against your needing an emergency kit, but when you do, you'll be immensely thankful for it. Two specialized emergency items are wise additions in many situations.

Avalanche cord. If you are skiing in mountainous terrain, carry one; the standard avalanche cord is light nylon, about 50 feet long, and usually red. If you're caught in an avalanche and trailing one of these, it will normally be carried to the surface and allow rescuers to reach you quickly.

Aluminum shovel. A lightweight shovel is all you need to dig a good snow cave if you're skiing country where it's possible. These can be outstanding shelters; even when it's well below zero outside, the temperature in a cave will stay right around freezing. (See Chapter 7 for the full rundown on snow caves.)

So much for the tour leader's rucksack, even on a one-day jaunt. Though the list here is long and may seem formidable, it's surprising how light and compact this collection can be made with a little looking, testing, and juggling. In addition, there's a certain satisfaction in getting these items together and knowing they will pull you through any situation. Finally, all this gear serves as psychological insurance: it's there; you don't have to worry about being caught unprepared; you can enjoy the tour instead. Finally, don't let that term "tour leader" be deceiving; you might find yourself in this role much sooner than you expect.

In a normal party it's unnecessary for everyone to tote the bag of tricks just described. But each person should carry his own basic provisions and clothing, plus some back-up items as well. Here's a much simpler list for each member of the tour other than the leader:

- **All layers of clothing that you're not wearing**
- **An extra pair of gloves**
- **An extra pair of socks**
- **Your own lunch and something to drink**
- **Sunburn lotion and chapstick**
- **Sunglasses** (or in certain situations, goggles)
- **Avalanche cord** (if you're in the mountains)
- **Warm hat** (if not on your head)
- **Emergency kit** (You should never separate from the party, but on rare occasions, it can't be helped; your own emergency kit is for such occasions.)

That's it for the contents of your rucksack. Think about this: chances are you've just read the most important section of this book.

PUTTING IT TOGETHER

Knowing what to carry, and being sure to carry it, is an essential preface to all tours—no matter where or how long. This is pretty much fixed information; you don't want to be casual about the contents of your pack; you want to be sure instead.

The tour itself is an entirely different matter; there are numerous dimensions and directions, with relatively few hard and fast checkpoints anywhere in sight. Here are a few guidelines to send you on your way.

Where to Tour

This is one of the most wonderful things about touring. You tour where there is snow, and that can be just about anywhere. In the winter of 1972-1973, a succession of freak storms actually made it possible to ski tour in Utah's Canyonlands National Park; that's desert country better known for its cactus blooms, sand stone pinnacles, and heat. There have also been flurries of touring activity in New York's Central Park. Repeat: only the snow limits where you tour.

Time out for ice fishing.

More practically, you will, at least to start with, want to seek out marked, and perhaps even groomed and maintained trails. To go into these in any detail would make for another whole book—or more likely a multi-volume set. Robert Colwell's *Guide to Snow Trails* (Stackpole Books, 1973) is an excellent place to start; it covers the entire United States with well-annotated listings of just about every touring center and trail complex of major consequence. If you want further information, chances are you'll find it in any one of a growing number of regional or state guidebooks. Here are a few to start with.

• Rudolph Mattesich, editor, *Ski Touring Guide* (The Ski Touring Council, Troy, VT). An annual publication of ski tours in the East.

• Robert D. Larson, *Ski Touring Handbook* (Central Division, U.S. Ski Association, Chicago, IL, 1972). A general guide for the upper Midwest.

• Morgan Queal, editor, *A Guide to Ski Touring* (Rocky Mountain Division, U.S. Ski Association, Denver, CO, 1972). Covering Colorado, southern Wyoming, and New Mexico.

• David Beck, *Ski Tours in California* (Far West Ski Association, San Francisco, CA, 1972).

• Doug Newman and Sally Sharrard, *Oregon Ski Tours* (1973).

The list could go on. If your area isn't covered here, check out the bookshelves of the local touring shops. New volumes of this kind are rolling off the presses at a steady rate.

If you're not interested in books, then find out where to tour by asking around. Logical places to check are nearby alpine ski areas or touring centers, national forest or park offices, local clubs, and touring shops. For finer details, it's always wise to carry a United States Geological Survey map of the area you're touring (unless it's well-marked and defined).

Finding Company

Until you're reasonably at home on skis and with the winter, it's best to hitch on with a group tour led by an experienced and knowledgeable hand. The approach here is the same as for locating good places to tour. Again, check the following: nearby alpine ski areas and touring centers, local clubs, touring shops, and guides and outfitters running winter trips.

The inevitable wineskin: not an essential.

Doing it Yourself

The time may soon come when you want to head out on your own tour with a couple of friends. A few pointers will handle this here (for fuller details on tour leadership, see Chapter 8).

● Know the route, or have someone along who does. Failing this, do some thorough asking around about it, and obviously have a map; when you're exploring new country always proceed with extra caution. Whatever the case, settle on a route and stay with it unless there is a pressing reason for a change. A good day's tour will always be helped by variety; the route should wind through diverse country—sometimes in the woods, sometimes in the open, and so forth. If the trail is a loop, so much the better; you'll be traveling through continually new country. If it's possible to plan a reasonable mix of uphills, downhills, and flat stretches, do it. Know your own ability and those of everyone in your group; don't plan a tour that overtaxes anyone.

• Always let someone who remains behind know your route, your destination and when you expect to return. If you get into trouble, a search and rescue party can be dispatched to help you home. Registration boxes are placed at trailheads in many national parks, national forests and other popular areas; the rule here is to sign in and sign out. Rangers check the lists regularly; if anything goes wrong, it's soon checked out.

• Plan for contingencies. Are you ready for unexpected storms or bad weather? If someone gets hurt, can you handle it? Who goes for help? Whom do they contact? Do you know the search and rescue unit in your area? Are the members reliable? Obviously you don't want any of these things to happen; however, you also want to be sure to deal with them if they do.

7

The Overnight Tour

In Europe, it's common for families or groups to head out on overnight tours. In both the Alps and Scandinavia the touring trail is dotted with huts, many of them fully staffed, where one can warm his toes, eat a hearty supper, spend the night, have breakfast, pick up a trail lunch and then ski all day to the next hut.

Hut-hopping, as some call it, has plenty of merit. With little more than a well-stocked day pack on his back, one can ski steadily and easily for weeks. On this side of the Atlantic the concept is not that developed. True, American hut systems do exist: the famous Appalachian Mountain Club huts in New Hampshire's White Mountains (some now open for tour skiers); the four United States Ski Association huts above the Castle Creek Valley near Aspen, Colorado; others scattered across the continent from the Adirondacks to the Cascades and north into the Canadian Rockies. These are very much the exception, though the concept (especially when the huts are geared for both summer hiking and winter touring) is slowly attracting greater interest in a variety of circles.

115

View from the tent.

Thus, if one wants to spend more than a day on skis, it's likely he'll find himself in the business of snow camping on his overnight sojourns. Except for some brief, teeth-rattling moments first thing in the morning, it's a much more pleasant experience than the uninitiated would dare believe. Furthermore, the benefits can be magnificent. Camping spots that in the summer are crowded become havens of quiet from November into early spring. The opportunity to explore more remote wilderness areas can turn warm season pursuits into year-round exploration.

As with the day tour, the joys of extended tours in the wilds rapidly become self-evident as you ski along. The rest of this chapter will take those for granted, and focus on those cautionary elements and handy tricks that make life in the snow both safer and more pleasant.

WHAT TO CARRY

The basic principle of the day tour applies to the over-nighter as well: carry what you need to deal with whatever might go wrong, and to prevent anything from going wrong in the first place. Extended tours mean prolonged exposure to whatever the winter weather chooses to cook up and throw at you. It pays to have ample warm clothing and also a good supply of back-up gear.

Group Gear

As on the day tour, one member of the overnight party will function as the leader. Sometimes this follows the same pattern as the day tour, with one person heading a group of followers who have signed on for the tour. Frequently, a group of compatible and about equally competent skiers will head out together—none of them really functioning as the leader in an overtly acknowledged sense. In this case, it's still wise to have one member of the party act as ramrod or school marm, not only to be sure that all necessary gear is aboard, but to know also who is carrying what. Here's a basic list.

- **Repair kit.** The same as on a day tour. This is essentially a group (or leader's) item, though individuals may want to carry a few extra items of their own (for example, an extra ski tip, or perhaps some tape).
- **First Aid Kit.** On a longer trip, it's wise to expand the basic day tour kit at least slightly. Among the additions to consider are salt tablets, treatment for rashes and chafing, eye medication, and narcotics and antibiotics (if one is qualified to use them). Many summer backpackers, knowing their own peculiar susceptibilities, carry personal first aid supplements; the prescription for overnight or multiday winter tours should be no different. In the winter, especially, it pays to be ready for all contingencies. First aid supplies—bandages, pills, a syringe or medicine—weigh precious little when compared to their great potential value.
- **Food.** The lightweight results of the freeze-dried

revolution work just as well in winter as in summer. On a snow tour, however, emphasis on higher caloric output is strongly advised. Parties should also carry an extra day's provisions as a matter of common practice; an unexpected storm can quickly prolong a trip beyond its expected limits.

The food is almost always divided among the members of the party. Since fishing through packs for the various ingredients of a meal can be a chore in the cold, menus are often planned and packed (plastic sacks do just fine) in advance. In this way, it's assured that one person is carrying Tuesday's lunch and supper, while another is carrying Wednesday's breakfast. Each individual should carry his own ample supply of trail snacks, again with the emphasis on high energy foods (raisins, nuts, chocolate chips, jerky, etc.).

• **Cookware and Stove.** These are normally divvied up as part of the food. The nesting aluminum pots (usually in sets of three or four) are standard ware both for backpackers and skiers. Some of these are unnecessarily heavy, so if you're shopping around, bear this in mind. Models with covers are especially important in the winter; they conserve heat and speed up cooking. A large spoon and a scouring pad and/or some biodegradable soap (Dr. Bonner's backpacking soap is great) are all that are necessary for the group. Individuals will want to carry their own cups (preferably plastic; hot drinks chill more quickly in a metal cup), plus a spoon and fork.

The lightweight backpacking stoves are even more valuable on the overnighter than they are for a day tour. Unless you find an open stream, you'll depend on the stove, not only for cooking, but also for melting snow to water. Pump models are preferable for cold weather use. Larger groups may want to use heavier units like the Phoebus 625; it weighs 2½ pounds but is powerful enough to cook for from six to eight people. When in use, set the stove on a small foam pad or something similar; otherwise it's apt to melt the snow beneath it and sink out of sight.

- **Other Group Gear.** On the overnight tour, it's often wise to carry extras of items that only the tour leader would ordinarily worry about on the day run. More than one map and compass is advisable for a party any larger than four or five. If you plan to dig snow caves, have at least two aluminum shovels along. For the rest, members of the party should carry the same basic back-up gear as on the day tour; again, be sure you know who has what, and have items that might be needed in a hurry readily accessible (not buried in the bottom of someone's pack).

Individual Gear

If you have done any summer backpacking, all you'll have to do for snow camping is beef up some of your equipment for added warmth, and perhaps add a few items.

The Pack. If you have a decent summer backpack, use it, but with one caution. Modern hiking packs are designed to carry weight fairly high on the shoulders; for the hiker, this is fine, but it can make the skier top-heavy and trouble his balance. Loading the pack so its center of gravity is as low as possible will partially compensate for this, but the real solution here lies in improved touring technique. Downhill running usually presents the greatest challenge to the heavily loaded skier. The tendency is inadvertently to let the pack push you forward or pull you back.

The larger touring rucksacks are designed with balance in mind; their profiles are trimmer (often with mountaineering needs in mind), but few are roomy enough for the gear one inevitably needs on extended trips. The French Sacs Millet (marketed in the United States by Recreational Equipment, Inc. of Seattle), the new Holubar Royal Pack, Alp Sports Eiger Standard and Rivendell's Jensen wraparound pack (the largest) are representative quality units. The price range is from $30 to $50 for this group.

The Sleeping Bag. A good down-filled model is a must; make sure there's plenty of quality goose down. Depending on the style and construction of the bag, 2½ pounds will keep you warm from zero to 20-degrees below. This will probably cost you in the neighborhood of $100; if well taken care of, that's a minimum 10-year investment, unless you're really using it heavily.

Though goose down is by far the most popular fill material for sleeping bags (and parkas, mitts, boots, etc.), there are those who staunchly maintain that dacron-type synthetics are superior. The resulting debate seems destined to drag on for decades without a winner, and certainly no attempt will be made to settle the issue here. A list of the benefits of each fill material indicates that both are generally up to the job of keeping you warm in winter.

Down: excellent warmth; lightweight; breathable; compressible; resilient. It is also expensive (as with skis, the price of natural materials is rising faster than that of synthetics; raw down is going up 15 percent annually). Goose down is useless when wet; insulating properties drop near zero, and weight soars.

Dacron (For example, DuPont's Fiberfill II): less expensive; retains loft and insulating qualities when wet; much more easily dried than down. It is not as compressible, and somewhat heavier.

Whatever bag you select should be on the roomy side, not one of those tight-fitting mummy models; on cold nights (which are most nights) you'll want to pull some of your gear inside the bag with you. This is especially so of your boots; the idea of sleeping with shoes may sound odd, but it also keeps them warm and avoids the unpleasant experience of putting on cold frozen boots in the morning.

In addition to the bag, you'll want a foam pad between you and the snow. Closed-cell Ensolite insulates well, is light and compact when rolled; a half-inch thickness will more than take care of snow camping situations. A full length pad is unnecessary; a sweater or other item of clothing under the feet will take care of insulation against the snow down there.

Clothing. The demands for clothing on an overnight tour can extend beyond the considerations of the layer principle of the day trip. On these longer trips, there will simply be more time when you're out in the snow, but not skiing, not exercising to stay warm. Many people bring along a down (or Fiberfill) sweater or parka for the evenings and first thing in the morning. Down booties are also handy.

Depending on the length of the tour, you will want to bring ample changes of clothing, particularly underwear and socks. Even more important than the obvious matter of basic pleasantness, clean clothing is invariably warm clothing. Socks, for example, should not be worn longer than a couple of days; beyond that their insulating properties diminish too much.

SHELTER

When it comes to shelter, winter campers have a distinct advantage over summertime backpackers because of the abundant presence of a raw material called snow. It's an excellent insulator, and usually has good structural properties as well. Its presence makes possible a surprising variety of shelters. With a shovel, skis and poles, and sometimes pine boughs, two people can build a warm, albeit impromptu, bivouac shelter in no more than 30 minutes. Snow caves and igloos require more time, but are remarkably warm and quiet.

Tents

For those who want to carry the extra weight, or who ski in country where the snow is comparatively scant, a number of winter expedition tents are available. Even the best expedition tent is seldom as warm as a snow cave, but it does have other advantages. In some areas, where the snow cover is shallow or not reasonably packed, the tent is your only serious choice.

Once you master its idiosyncrasies, a tent can also be

pitched in five or ten minutes, and be taken down just as quickly—a major gain if you are moving camp from one night to the next, and do not want to take the time to dig snow caves.

Tent design should be such that it catches as little wind as possible (flapping tents can mean sleepless nights) and also sheds the snow. A model with a vestibule is advised for two reasons: first you can stash your packs out of the elements; second, you can usually brush most of the snow off of you in the vestibule, rather than bringing it in onto the bags, dry clothing, etc. Another handy addition is the frost liner, usually made of muslin or a cotton-dacron blend, which hangs along the walls and roof inside the tent. This will provide greater warmth, and also ease condensation problems (a layer of frost on the inside of the tent in the morning can be unpleasant, especially when some of it dumps down your neck).

Like a good winter sleeping bag, a cold weather tent is expensive; the Sierra Designs Glacier Tent and the Holubar Expedition tent, both two-man (or tight three-man) models, run near $150.00, with the frost liner an extra $25.00. The Gerry Himalayan, which comes complete with everything including fiber glass stays to stabilize the walls, sells for $250.00. Though these tents will weigh more than straight summer models, that's the only consideration that might make you shy away from using one of these tents year-round.

Pitching a tent in the snow requires a few special techniques. For the floor, stamp down an even patch of snow. Do not waste time digging down to bare ground; it will be frozen and colder than the snow. To anchor the guy ropes, use a tree when possible; otherwise improvise or carry some kind of an anchor. A ski buried in the snow will usually anchor the ropes amply; even more effective is a snow fluke, which is nothing more than a large lightweight aluminum flange that, when pushed into the snow at an angle, serves as a good, firm anchor.

Snow Caves

For those who've never done it, digging and sleeping in a snow cave will be an unexpected delight. Design possibilities are almost limitless, and once completed, these natural shelters maintain a temperature right around freezing; in addition, they are extraordinarily quiet even with a raging gale just outside.

Two views of a snow cave, outside and in.

The important thing in digging a snow cave is to find the right place for it. In many parts of the United States, this is no problem at all. A large, wind-packed drift is the ideal spot, but anywhere the snow is well settled will suffice. Snow depth and firmness are the only criteria that must be met; all you need is enough room for the cave, and snow that will stand up.

A tough, lightweight aluminum shovel does just fine for the digging. Start out with a small entrance into the side of the drift—large enough for a person to crawl through and no more. Whenever possible, tunnel in horizontally, or even at a slight angle upward. This not only makes the job easier (less stooping and bending) as you dig the cave, but eliminates the possibility of colder air becoming trapped in a low pocket.

Once you tunnel in three or four feet (or more if you wish, or if the shape of the drift requires it), all you do is hollow out a room large enough for your needs. Some people insist that the roof should be arched for greater support; this is a good idea, but not necessary in solid snow. In truth, unless you're an architectural nut, you'll probably dig a dome-shaped room as a matter of course anyway.

Two helpful tips while digging:
- Wear a raincoat or something that will keep you dry. No matter how cold it is, digging a snow cave is a wet operation; if it's above freezing, you can get drenched in a hurry. Some people also use plastic sacks (for example, a bread wrapper) over their hands to avoid coping with a pair of well-soaked gloves.
- Two people can dig a cave at least three times faster than one person alone. After the entrance, which is a one-man job, have one person inside working on the cave, while the other stands outside and clears the accumulating snow away from the entrance. It will save on stiff muscles (especially in the back) if you switch positions once in a while.

The completed snow cave can take on any number of shapes. It should be high enough so you can at least kneel easily without knocking a shower of snow off the roof, and inevitably down your neck. Many people like to level off raised ledges or platforms for sleeping—to avoid the cold which settles in the low spots, and for something more comfortable to sit on. *Be absolutely sure to poke a breathing and ventilation hole in the roof;* the best spot is directly above where you'll do the cooking. Other embellishments are optional; shelves for gear can be hollowed from the walls, and additional rooms dug as needed. For those who always longed for snow castles when they were children, this is the perfect way to fulfill that dream.

This is the standard cave, but there are plenty of variations. Sometimes it's sufficient just to dig a narrow slit on the lee side of a drift and then tuck your bag in there. If no drifts can be found, and the snow depth and pack are sufficient, you can sink a vertical shaft into the level snow and then hollow out a room off from it. A very quick and effective one-man storm shelter is possible if the snow is firm enough so that it can be cut into blocks. Simply shovel out (or stamp down) a rectangular space in the snow large enough for you and your sleeping bag (seven feet by three, by one and a half deep is plenty); then cut and lay a course or two of blocks around the perimeter leaving one end open; place your skis lengthwise and poles crosswise over the blocks as roof supports, and then lay a final course over the top. Thereafter, crawl in the open end with your gear and pull a last block in place behind you. This shelter works especially well in wind-blown country where blowing snow will fill in the cracks between the blocks. It won't be roomy, but it will be snug. In many parts of the United States, the snow doesn't pack hard enough to make block shelters like this; however if the opportunity presents itself, it's usually quicker than digging a cave.

As far as actually living in a snow cave (or snow shelter of any kind) is concerned, there are a few simple precautions.

- Be sure to bring along a waterproof ground cloth to put under your foam pad; it will make for a much drier and warmer stay.

- A candle or backpack stove will warm a snow cave surprisingly; the candle will also supply plenty of light. Just be sure the shelter is well ventilated, and do not leave anything burning after you turn in for the night. Though it's not likely that you'll suffocate, your oxygen supply will be depleted with a resulting hangover the following morning. If it is snowing, check periodically to be sure the vent hole doesn't plug up.

- Bring all your gear inside with you (especially the shovel); if it snows during the night, nothing will be buried and lost (and if it really snows, you can dig your way out). Stand skis and poles vertically in the snow outside.

- If you're using a snow cave as a base camp for day tours, be sure it is well marked so you can find it upon your return. In the mountains, one drift can look pretty much like another.

In the end, the real key to effective winter snow shelter is ingenuity. As long as you allow yourself an hour or two of working light at the end of a day for construction, there's just no reason for you ever having to spend a winter's night in the open.

FIRES

On a longer trip, a campfire or two will probably be necessary—if not for warming up, then almost certainly for drying out. Winter campfires seldom pose any hazard, but there is the problem of how to keep a blaze going *on top* of the snow (a fire that sinks down 2 or 3 feet is awkward at first, and then increasingly useless). If there's no place where you can dig down to bare ground for your fire, cut a platform of green logs and build the blaze atop that. Don't build fires under overhanging trees; falling snow from the branches can extinguish your efforts in a puff.

View from the edge of a glacier—a long, overnight expedition in the Wind River Range, Wyoming.

PUTTING IT TOGETHER

The basic principles for planning a day tour apply to the over-night tour as well. The only difference is one of degree. On the day tour, you plan a simple route; whereas on the overnighter, you're really talking a full-scale itinerary. It's wise to plan this carefully and in detail. Have alternative routes available in case your planned path turns out to be blocked or otherwise imprac-tical. If you're heading out for any extended period, it's wise to allow for a layover day about halfway along—not only for a rest, but also to consolidate, reorganize, and redistribute gear. The ideal layover spot is one from which a modest day tour can be launched to a scenic spot, a mountain summit or a good downhill run.

Choosing members of the party becomes much more im-portant on a longer tour. Psychological rough edges generally don't develop in a day; however, a week or so of close inter-dependence in tight quarters can bring out both the bad and the good of a group rather sharply. It pays to know who you're skiing with, and how they react not just to extreme stress, but more significantly, to the normal wear and tear of fatigue, damp clothing, plain hard work, etc. Few extended tours are de-signed to be trials by winter, but the possibility of being holed up by a storm, or something else, for a day or longer, increases with the length of the trip. Some classic, and often trying, outdoor dramas have developed under just these circum-stances.

8

The Complete Tour Leader

The title of this chapter may be a mistake. If you get hung up on that word "leader" and think, "Well this is for some pro, certainly not me," then stop right there. This chapter is for everyone. Even if you never lead a tour, it's wise to know the responsibilities of those who do. Furthermore, many people who don't expect to be leading a tour often end up in just that position. As has been said before: if you're unwisely touring alone, you're the leader; if two people are touring together, one must be the leader.

Across the United States the group tour is becoming increasingly popular. The variety offered is amazing, as is the range of companies offering them. Every major touring center has its special trails and regular trips. Even the comparatively small operation—lodge, shop, or local club—might lead groups into the hills every weekend from November through April, with daily runs often available (see Appendix B for a list of some of the major touring and instructional centers in the United States).

129

eping the group together in the Cariboos
the Canadian Rockies.

Most people join a tour for no more than two simple reasons. They want a guided introduction to an unfamiliar patch of territory, or to a familiar summer hiking haunt now under the guise of winter. Tour skiers also want to enjoy themselves with a congenial group of people. It matters not whether there are three skiers or twenty; the rationale for joining a tour seldom varies.

A group tour, just like any other group activity, has its own special dynamics; there are front-runners and followers, go-getters and laggards. Out in the snow on a tour, these personality nuances should be kept in line for the overall good of the group—especially that of its less conditioned and experienced members. A single fatigued, sunburned, cramped, or otherwise weakened person can quickly jeopardize the day for twenty others. One cannot repeat this too much: winter conditions reduce one's margin of error—whether that "one" be you, alone, or a troop of twenty-five skiers.

The tour leader *must* be acutely aware of the following guidelines. If any of these concerns are beyond your range, don't try to lead a tour; it's just not good sense. Even if you're gliding along back in the ranks, however, it's wise to bear these matters generally in mind. By doing so, you'll probably help the leader, and thereby improve the overall quality of the tour.

In the High Sierras of California above Lake Tahoe. If you ski alone, you're the leader.

LET THE LEADER LEAD

Without being militaristic, the tour leader should be *the one* in charge of the trip and the well-being of the entire group. Many professionals in the tour business say their greatest problem is the skier who will not follow the leader's direction. In no time at all, this can turn a heretofore enjoyable trip into a divisive, uncertain journey. If you join a tour, accept the presence of the leader as a *fait accompli* before you start out and take his or her word throughout. If the leader is not to your liking, you do not have to tour with the tour operator again.

DECIDE WHO CARRIES WHAT

First of all, everyone should tote his own basic gear whether the person who skis is on a casual two-hour jaunt, or a strenuous two-week expedition. There's always that remote chance of separation, accidental or forced, and you want to be able to handle it with confidence. The tour leader will also carry repair and first aid kits, plus other special equipment (see Chapter 6).

There is sometimes a tendency to convert the tour leader into a hired pack mule or a porter; he ends up lugging extra sweaters, lunches, thermoses, and whatnot. The practice may have a certain snob appeal, but it's not wise. Carry your own gear, and chances are you'll feel more a part of the group.

This does not mean that everyone should carry the same weight. The group equipment (on a longer trip, this means the food, the cookware, the stove, the tent, etc.) should be distributed among the stronger members of the party. One or two may carry none of this at all. The point is simply to load each person so he can keep comfortable pace with everyone else. A general rule in the loading process is: if weight becomes a problem, leave unnecessary items behind. For some people, this could mean leaving the camera in the car; for others, it could mean bringing the camera, but not the tripod and extra lenses. Never scrimp on essentials; if you think you *might* need that extra pair of socks, then by all means bring them.

ADJUST THE GROUP PACE

No aspect of a group tour is more vital, and often more subtle than the pace. There is only one good pace for the tour; it's the one at which everyone is gliding along with the group, without excess effort. Only rarely can you go too slow; all too easily you can go too fast.

The best pattern for a tour is one with fairly frequent stops—resting, enjoying a view, taking pictures, examining animal tracks, waxing, or munching a candy bar. If a skier happens to lag behind (usually, this should not happen), stop and let him catch up; then let him have time to rest. There's no hurry; forced marches are not part of the touring sport.

In handling pace, a leader's problems will almost always come from the extremes: the spring chicken who insists on charging ahead; and the inexperienced or less conditioned skier who falls behind. It's tough to say which is easier to cope with. The hard-charging type can sometimes upset the pace of

Maintaining an easy pace up MacMillan Peak in southwestern Colorado.

the entire group, break down its unity, and cause all kinds of spin-off troubles. He may, for example, be the reason three people at the end of the line are puffing and wearing thin. If possible, divert his attention to something that will slow him down; if you can do this without his knowing your motive, so much the better. The person who begins to drag usually presents a simpler problem. Get him off the end of the line (back there the pace is often a bit jerky) up into position near the head of the line so you can control the pace of the entire group according to his condition. With either of these types, act earlier rather than later; you're best off when you move immediately.

The best time to deal with overzealous pace is in the first five minutes of the tour. That's normally when the more energetic skiers will want to boom ahead; if they can be reined in early, then a relaxed rhythm will take over and generally maintain itself for the entire duration of the journey. A less conditioned or experienced skier can begin to drag at any time, though his problems are most apt to occur late in the morning (before lunch and the accompanying rest) or afternoon. Slowing down the pace and stepping up the number of breaks are the obvious means for easing a tired skier back to home base. Offering extra, high-energy trail snacks, plus something to drink, will also help; fatigue and dehydration are what commonly make a lagging skier.

One very important aspect of maintaining a suitable pace is sizing up the abilities of those in your group. This you must do by acute observing; there are too many times when it's unwise to take a person's word about his fitness or skill. Before the start or during those early minutes of the tour are the times for evaluation; you can often spot a skier whose lack of technique is apt to wear him down later in the day. The most unpleasant task that falls on a tour leader is to tell a person to stay home. However, this is sometimes necessary for the good of the group. It is much better to avoid a problem by anticipating, rather than having to solve it by reacting.

The good tour leader is always vigilant about pace. He *feels* the people behind him—knows almost intuitively if they're moving easily along, or having to work.

AVOID SEPARATION

The touring group should be a relaxed organism; you should ski when it skis and stop when it stops. The person who repeatedly veers out of line to take pictures can disrupt a tour in a hurry. Invariably he falls behind and must press to catch up. There is also the chronic digressor: the person, who with the most genuine interest, wanders off to look at a tree, watch a bird or peer over a rise. For him, staying with the group can be frustrating; if possible, turn the group to his interests, or slow it for some other purpose to a modest, but not overly accommodating, degree.

KNOW THE ROUTE

Any uncertainty about the route—its precise course or its distance—spells trouble. A competent leader has skied his touring country literally dozens of times; he knows the distances, the terrain, the possible hazards, the sheltered stopping places, the special sights, and just about anything else that might occur along the way. He knows alternative courses to take should unexpected obstacles occur. If a sudden spring thaw has opened up a stream, and made it impossible to cross, for example, he can reroute the group safely and sensibly without much more than a moment's hesitation. Nothing less will do.

(Exploring a new route, which can be both delightful and exciting, is obviously another matter. With any group that heads into new territory, the abilities of each member should be well established. All should understand that this is an exploration; there should be a steady sharing of observations about terrain, snow conditions, and how the skiers are holding up. On any exploratory tour, all members must assume a greater re-

Lining up behind the leader (not the dog) on Steamboat Lake, Colorado.

sponsibility for the well-being of the group. Always have a good map and compass; if possible, ask about the country beforehand, of people who *do* know it.)

PLAN FOR TIME AND DISTANCE

Most tours will cover just about *a mile an hour*, though this can vary considerably with the terrain, the snow, and the weather. That means the average day's run (with close to an hour out for lunch) probably won't cover more than five or six miles. If you go beyond that, you probably have either a predominance of downhill grades or a group of proven, hardy skiers. No one in the tour group should be exhausted at the end of the day; aim instead for a pleasantly tired exhilaration.

It's wise to plan to end the tour a good two hours before sunset, even on the shortest winter days (and, remember, those days are short, especially in December and January). If you encounter unexpected problems en route, chances are you'll be able to work them out in daylight, before the chill of night sets in.

If you see you'll be overtaken by sundown, assess your situation very carefully. An overnight bivouac need not be uncomfortable, and it is much safer than trying to grope your way out in the dark—risking unseen hazards, dangerous fatigue and increased possibilities of becoming lost. In avalanche country, night travel is pure folly.

USE COMMON SENSE

This applies to everything, and salt in some prudent caution while you're at it. It is better to turn back than press on to a destination at any cost. Ski touring is not a sport for making heroes. Stop and rest a few extra times if there's any hint of weariness. Be alert for any danger signs—anywhere, with anyone. Be sure that people are enjoying themselves.

9
The World Out There (When Winter Turns Mean)

Winter is beautiful. The ski touring boom would not have occurred unless this were incredibly so. For those who have ventured out onto the snow, beauty may take on an infinity of forms. The almost overwhelming quiet. The willy-nilly tracings of animal tracks. The delicate play of long shadows over unbroken snow. The dazzling aftermath of a heavy frost. The awesome outline of whitened peaks etched hard against a brittle blue sky. No person needs to be told of these; all are out there for one to discover and enjoy for himself.

Winter can also be harsh, and sometimes downright savage.

Plan carefully, and you'll rarely encounter those severe conditions that are talked about a good deal more than actually experienced. But even though winter turns mean less often than one would think, it's always wise to know what *might* happen and how to deal with it. Harsh winter conditions cut quickly into one's margin of safety; you should be able to deal with all contingencies.

This chapter and the next deal with the sometime fury of winter from two different angles. In this chapter, the focus will be on natural conditions and their potential dangers. In the next chapter, attention will turn to methods of dealing with this harsher side of winter should the need arise.

Basically, there are but two kinds of wintertime hazards: those caused by snow (or ice) on the ground and those caused by the weather. Nothing else could go wrong.

AVALANCHES

The study of snow is a science in itself, and the study of avalanches is a major part of it. The University of Colorado's Institute of Arctic and Alpine Research (INSTAAR) has been probing the hows and whys of the avalanche for years, as has the United States Forest Service's Avalanche Study Center at Alta, Utah. Both have delved deeply into the intricacies of snow crystal formation, the changes those crystals undergo on the ground (called metamorphism), the mechanical properties of

The Irene Avalanche cuts loose near Silverton, Colorado.

the snow cover, and those special, often mysterious, conditions that trigger an avalanche and send it hurtling down a slope at speeds up to 240 mph.

The racer does not need to concern himself about avalanches at all; his track does not reach into hazard areas. The light tour skier who sticks to well-laid-out and patrolled trails seldom has any worry either. The tour skier who heads into the high country and the ski mountaineer, however, should be constantly alert.

The best way to stay out of avalanche trouble is to steer clear of avalanche areas. Throughout the national forests and parks of the West, avalanche histories have been fairly well documented. In some regions this history goes well back in time—far before anyone ever thought of studying them. For example, the lofty San Juan Mountains of southwestern Colorado boast a number of known avalanche paths first (and sometimes disastrously) discovered by nineteenth-century gold and silver miners; the more notorious of these are even named in the colorful spirit characteristic of that era: Mother Kline, Irene, Slippery Jim, Black Widow, Grizzly, and Happy End, to note a few. Tour skiers in the San Juans simply regard these avalanche zones as off-limits (unfortunate in that it closes off much of these magnificent mountains to their wanderings, but also unmistakably wise).

Here, as elsewhere in the West, the Forest Service has posted many signs noting avalanche areas; though with more and more skiers cutting tracks into the hills, the agency has been hard pressed to keep up. If you're planning to head into any area that you think might possibly be avalanche country, the sensible thing is to check at the nearest Forest Service District Ranger's office. Since this agency's districts are not that large, you'll probably find one within no more than 30 or 40 miles. National park headquarters or ranger stations serve the same purpose. In some heavily used areas, snow rangers blast avalanches loose with howitzers, or hand placed charges, before the snow piles up enough to inflict real damage on some unsuspecting passer-by. In other places (Yosemite National Park is one), rangers issue avalanche forecasts just as one does for the weather.

Many routes unavoidably take the tour skier and the mountaineer into avalanche country; so some brief commentary is in order.

Basic Definitions

Avalanches happen when the weight of the snow on a slope becomes too great for whatever is holding it in place. All avalanches fall into one of two basic categories. *Loose snow avalanches* occur most often when a fresh fall piles up in a bulk too great for the natural angle of repose. They usually begin at a point and fan out from there, gathering more snow as they build in force and speed. *Slab avalanches* are less predictable and more complex and they pose the greatest winter danger in the mountains and claim the largest number of victims. Slab avalanches involve large blocks, or masses, of fairly cohesive snow that break loose as a block and build from there; they are difficult to spot as they cannot be related to any particular snow type or visible property. Wind-packed snow often forms unstable slabs; the only way to understand the many variable causes of slab avalanches is to delve into the special intricacies of snow physics. Skiers caught in slab avalanches usually trigger the slides themselves; anything from a sonic boom to a snowshoe rabbit to changes within the slab can do the same.

Basic Precautions

Many half-true generalizations have been written of avalanches, but few overall statements can be made. It's often said that avalanches are confined to open slopes, and that one can consider himself safe if he's among trees. This is usually so, but not always; a scattering of timber may be insufficient to hold the snow (once under way, an avalanche can treat a stand of pines like so many matchsticks).

The following is not a list of infallible suggestions. None should be considered substitutes for caution, careful observation and general alertness. However, these general safety guidelines may save your life.

- Never travel alone in avalanche country.
- Whenever possible, detour around slide areas.
- The best detour is usually above the avalanche zone—for example, along the crest of a ridge.
- The greatest avalanche danger usually exists during and immediately after a heavy snowfall, or a prolonged spell of strong wind.
- Dangerous avalanches occur most often on slopes between 25° and 45°. At lower pitches, slides are less apt to break loose; at higher pitches, the snow tends to run before a heavy build up.
- If you must cross an avalanche path, never expose more than one member of the party at a time to the danger. Survivors can always begin rescue work immediately.

Scanning the Cardiac Ridge avalanche path from a respectful distance—near Alta, Utah.

• When deciding to cross a possible avalanche area, try to figure out what will happen should you be caught in a slide. If it seems possible you'll be swept over a cliff or buried in a gulch, don't go. Avalanches themselves are very difficult to predict; what could happen if you're hit by one is more evident.

• When crossing an avalanche area, use any natural features that might help you. A rock outcrop or a stand of trees may well serve as a refuge in case of a slide.

• In crossing an avalanche area, be sure your ski bindings are loose, and carry your poles in your hand; in case of a slide you don't want to be tangled up with either. It's also wise to loosen the straps of your pack or rucksack so you can bail out in a hurry. If you're not wearing them, put on your hat and mittens, zip up your windbreaker, and tie the hood tight; if you're buried in snow, you'll be a lot warmer. Also, be sure to use an avalanche cord.

• If you're caught in an avalanche, jettison all your gear immediately; you may well not have time, but try. Thereafter, use a swimming motion or anything else that helps keep you more or less upright and above the flow of the snow. Struggle to avoid getting tumbled over and over so you lose all sense of which way is up or down. Then, as the slide slows, get one hand over your mouth and, if you're still oriented, reach up with the other as high as you can. In a recent southwestern Colorado incident, a teenage boy was quickly rescued because one finger was poking out of the snow.

• Many avalanches set up quickly after running; some become as hard as Portland cement. That hand over your mouth may give you all the breathing room you'll have. If you can move, and know which way is up, try digging out. If you can't, remain as calm as possible (not easy), and wait for rescue. Use your entire will to keep from panic, which saps your energies and uses up your oxygen more quickly.

If you have escaped the avalanche, first check to be sure all slide danger is past. Next carefully note the last place where you saw your comrade (use a pole, ski, or some solid object to mark that point so you do not lose track of it). Then make a rapid surface search. Time is now your greatest enemy; the odds of a person surviving for an hour are 50-50; thereafter, they drop even lower (though there are records of victims hanging on for as long as 72 hours). First look for the avalanche cord or any articles (mittens, etc.) that may have been carried to the surface. Check carefully around any irregularities in the terrain that might have caught the skier in his plunge. If these efforts fail, begin an orderly probing of the snow with ski poles (hold by the tip and push the handle down into the snow),skis,or best of all, a steel avalanche probe made especially for this purpose.

Unless help is close by, sending for a rescue party is probably a waste of time. Concentrate all efforts on a fast rescue; you are in a race against the clock. The history of avalanche rescue includes too many instances of survivors leaving the scene in panic to seek help when only a brief, orderly search would have quickly uncovered the victim.

When you find the buried party, dig him out as quickly as possible. Be sure his breathing is good; if not, use artificial respiration. Thereafter, commence with standard first aid procedures, treating shock and loss of body heat first.

Avalanches are a fascinating subject of study in themselves. If you want to dig into this further, check any of the following:

- Colin Fraser, *The Avalanche Enigma* (New York: Rand McNally, 1966).
- Dale Gallagher, *Snowy Torrents–Avalanche Accidents in the U.S., 1910-1966* (Alta, Utah: U.S. Forest Service Avalanche Study Center, 1967).
- Ronald Perla, *Modern Avalanche Rescue* (Alta, Utah: U.S. Forest Service Avalanche Study Center, 1968).
- E. R. LaChapelle, *The ABC of Avalanche Safety* (Denver: Colorado Outdoor Sports Corp., 1961).

If you plan much travel in avalanche country, reading about this subject is a must.

All right. This has been a grisly account. Don't let it scare you. After all, avalanches are a special hazard and can be completely avoided without seriously limiting the range of your wanderings. In many parts of the United States, you couldn't find an avalanche if you tried. This section is in this book for those who cannot resist the lure of the mountains. It's a beautiful urge, but succumb to it wisely.

GLACIERS

Glaciers in the United States are few and far between. The Wind River Range in Wyoming and the North Cascades in Washington have some, as do those lonely volcanic giants of the Pacific Northwest, such as Mt. Rainier. There's always Canada, Alaska or the Alps, of course.

For some, touring (or mountaineering) a glacier can be a special quest; a glacier's great mass and inexorable movement, in slow time, can impart an almost mystical quality.

Glacier skiing in the Cariboos in the Canadian Rockies. Stay back from that ice.

Two basic precautions should be taken in regard to glaciers:

- Don't fool around near the sheer lower end (the tongue, or snout) of a glacier. An inevitable law of these rivers of ice is that, at some point or another, huge chunks break off and crash down.
- Crevasses are dangerous. These are yawning cracks in the ice, great splits formed as the glacier inches over the terrain. Crevasses are not something you want to fall into. The wisest precaution is for the whole party to rope, which takes us beyond the province of this book. See the Sierra Club's *Wilderness Skiing*.

WEATHER

This section is for everyone. Beyond the obvious, there is little to say of winter weather. Chances are you've been smacked by a few good storms in your time, and you've combatted them by remaining inside. For the touring fraternity, this is the sanest approach—particularly since the world can be so beautiful that first morning afterward, right outside your back door.

If you are planning the multi-day tour, it's especially important to check the weather map. If there's a front that appears to be moving in, best hold off until it passes. However, in some parts of the country, in mountainous areas particularly, this is easier said than done; small, nasty storms can brew up in a matter of hours. Occasionally larger ones will break with equal unpredictability. Of the problems they pose, the following are the most serious.

Wind

Most winter travelers agree that wind is their worst enemy. Even on a moderately warm day, a stiff blow can produce a chill factor that is far below the thermometer reading. A 30 mph wind, when the thermometer reads 20 degrees, equals −18 degrees when the air is still. Any combination of wind and

On the verge of a white out. It's about time for a bivouac.

temperature that drops the chill factor below about −15 degrees is apt to pose danger to exposed skin.

Ground Blizzards and White Out

Wind-driven snow can make visibility a problem. Sometimes the flying particles merely sting the eyes; a good pair of goggles will take care of that. Under more extreme conditions, however, the blowing snow can be so thick that one can barely see the next person in line ahead of him—or maybe no further than the end of his arm. Skiing ahead under such conditions is generally folly; seek out a protected gully, hollow, or similar windbreak and hole up (if possible dig a snow cave; refer to Chapter 7) until the blasts subside enough for you to see your direction clearly. The survival gear in your rucksack will carry you through the interim. Sometimes merely dropping into a valley will ease conditions enough for you to continue. This same procedure is often advisable on a clear day when the wind is high and the lowered chill factor makes prolonged exposure unwise.

Humidity

Water conducts heat away from the body about 24 times more

readily than does dry air. Since the humidity normally increases with the coming of a storm (the phenomenon is particularly noticeable in the East, the Sierras, and the Pacific Northwest), this bears watching. Clothing can readily become damp, and it's also much easier to perspire; accelerated chilling can result from either, as the body heat is dissipated, or more precisely, conducted away by the moist air.

The best way to handle the nastier whims of winter weather is vigilance. Keep an eye on the sky, and if foul weather signs appear, exercise appropriate caution. Don't feel defeated if you decide to clear out before an oncoming storm; even if you can't come back after it blows out, there's always next weekend, another month, the following year.

SPRING CONDITIONS

As the touring season moves on into mid-March and then April, it's easy for skiers to relax their guard. The worst of winter has passed; the sun is bright and higher in the sky; the days are longer and the temperatures warmer. It's the most beautiful and pleasant time to be out on skis, but still also a time for certain precautions.

Rotten Snow

Warmer spring temperatures do strange things to a blanket of snow. The snow's crystalline structure breaks down, and the cover tends to lose its supportive qualities; deterioration often sets in beneath the surface, causing hollows and cavities that can be booby traps.

Skiing on rotten snow can be a tough, grueling experience. Sometimes you'll sink in up to your knees or deeper with every step you take. Often you're in that precarious position of not knowing whether the snow will hold you up (it seems to cave in unpredictably about every third step; the tension is exhausting and the uncertainty nerve-wracking). Occasionally you'll even be able to see the snow collapsing in saucer-like depressions around you. Don't fight conditions like these; it just isn't worth the effort. Confine your travel to those hours of the day when the snow is firm—usually from dawn until ten or so in the morning and late in the afternoon. During the warm part of the day, it's best simply to make camp, sit around, and enjoy the sun (though that must be done in moderation).

Icy Snow

During the warm spring hours, the snow can be rotten; during the colder parts of the day, it can also crust over and become downright icy. This fact should prompt careful route planning if you're out in the mountains. You want to be sure to avoid traverses on steep (or sometimes not so steep) side hills during those early morning hours when the surface is a sheet of ice. Even if your skis have steel edges, ice can be a precarious proposition; if you slip, it's all too easy to go whizzing downhill on your back or side with nothing to stop you, but the trees, boulders or creek below. Should you absolutely have to cross an icy sidehill, it's best to take off your skis and kick steps, one by one, across the crusted expanse; this is slow, tedious work, but also your safest choice.

Lakes, Streams and Creeks

In the spring these not only melt, but also become swollen with runoff. As a general rule, avoid the possibility of open water altogether; if you must cross a lake, be sure to check the ice carefully. Remember too, that on a particularly warm day, a creek or stream can be completely buried beneath a sure cover of snow in the morning, and an open, raging torrent that same afternoon. Plan your route accordingly.

Sun

The bright sun can be as much a part of the weather as the worst storm. It's natural to button up immediately against the wind or cold, but because the sun's effects are less immediate, they're often ignored until it's too late and you've started to burn up. Sunburn cream, chapstick, and sunglasses (on multi-day tours be sure these have side shields) are imperative. Carry them, and use them. You may not look particularly attractive with heavy cream smeared all over your face, but come evening, you'll be much more comfortable. Be especially careful on those hazy bright days when penetrating, diffused light is deceptively strong.

10

Safety
and Survival

One of the great selling points of the touring sport is its safety. Boosters rightly point out that the incidence of broken bones is negligible; with the wonderful freedom of movement in those touring bindings, snapping a leg is just about impossible. So far so good.

Statisticians also note that the few serious muscular or skeletal injuries known in the long annals of touring have almost all occurred as the result of a collision. Someone buzzes off the trail and smacks into a tree, rock or a similar immovable obstacle. This, too, is insignificant.

The real problem of safety in touring is not these few injuries. The dangers of the sport are not a result of the activity itself, but rather of its environment—the outdoors in winter.

In fact, one basic truism of touring for anyone venturing off the well-beaten track, is that he darn well ought to be an outdoorsman just as much as he is a skier. Being a capable outdoorsman really boils down to one, simple thing: dealing with anything the natural world might throw at you or anyone in your party.

country like this, the elements can brew
trouble in a hurry.

GETTING LOST

Unless the weather kicks up its heels, there's no valid excuse for getting lost. Careful preparation, and a proven ability with map and compass, should keep you out of trouble in all but the most unusual of circumstances. This is so even though usually distinct landmarks can often take on a confusing sameness under a blanket of white.

In order to become a certified touring instructor under the aegis of the Rocky Mountain Division of the United States Ski Association, all candidates must demonstrate their skill with a map and compass. Every year when exam time rolls around, more than a few overconfident souls invariably hang up on just this part of the course. Falsely convinced that they can find the way around in the hills under any circumstances, they discover too late that their abilities were less than they thought. Many others, who knock about in the woods a fair bit, have developed what they think is an unerring ability to sniff out the proper direction under any circumstances. They believe they can follow the sun or the stars in a pinch; some even maintain their intuitions are better than a compass. "Just keep your eyes open and you'll know where you're at," goes the common logic. This is not wise.

For better or for worse, the human animal is one of the very few that cannot reliably orient himself in nature. Birds, fish, most mammals (some say the house cat is an exception), and even insects, can all instinctively get themselves directionally attuned; unquestionably, the phenomenon of migration (done unerringly by hummingbirds, bats, lemmings, and butterflies) is the most remarkable testimony to this skill. Humans cannot count on it; many, in fact, are the unfortunate souls who can be hopelessly lost when barely two minutes and/or 50 yards from the nearest road. For some reason, people frequently are not programmed to travel in straight lines; if lost they commonly (and sometimes quite unconsciously) veer in circles.

The solution to his homing inability has come from technology—particularly that of the map and the compass. As has been noted earlier, the best of these are the United States Geological Survey maps, and the ingenious Silva compasses, which are specially designed for route finding. Furthermore, these two items have been brought together in a sport that now has a recreational as well as a practical basis.

GROUND-TO-AIR EMERGENCY CODE

Successful winter search and rescue from the air depends on the ability of the people on the ground to communicate their situation. The following symbols will do the job; pack them clearly in the snow, or use contrasting boughs and other debris. Each should be at least 20 feet long and in a large clearing where it can readily be seen.

I 1. REQUIRE DOCTOR	**II** 2. REQUIRE MEDICAL SUPPLIES	**X** 3. UNABLE TO PROCEED	**F** 4. REQUIRE FOOD & WATER
K 5. INDICATE DIRECTION TO PROCEED	**↑** 6. GOING THIS DIRECTION	**LL** 7. ALL WELL	**N** 8. NO
Y 9. YES	**⌐L** 10. NOT UNDER– STOOD	**□** 11. NEED COMPASS & MAP	**!** 12. NEED SIGNAL LAMP

Courtesy of Yosemite Mountaineering

The sport of orienteering was born in Sweden just after World War I, and has long since spread throughout Europe, where international championships, as well as many local events, are now held regularly. As a testimony to its seriousness, orienteering has been a compulsory subject in Swedish grammar schools since 1942; children are nine or ten when they first begin learning the skills of map reading and compass use. However, orienteering has been slower to catch on in the United States—perhaps because of a hangover from the pioneer era when explorers commonly followed their noses and relied on their eyes. Today, however, the sport is gaining steadily in popularity.

The surest way to avoid getting lost: check the map and use the compass.

Reduced to essentials, orienteering takes the necessity of survival (route finding), and turns it into a recreational pursuit; it's the same pattern long ago taken with swimming. The great virtue of the sport, aside from its pleasurable aspects, is that it teaches a solid skill with map and compass. One learns such things as the difference between true north and magnetic north, how to take map and field bearings, how to determine the course from point A to point B, and how to triangulate locations. In short, a good orienteer is just not going to get lost.

However, it's not necessary to get into the sport to develop this skill—just as long as you develop it. The Silva compasses (the company produces a variety of models) are all accompanied with lucid directions. If you really want to get into the sport, Silva's mentor in the United States, Bjorn Kjellstrom, has prepared an excellent book, *Be Expert with Map and Compass*, available both through many outdoor shops, and also directly from the company's American headquarters in LaPorte, Indiana.

A U.S. Geological Survey map and Silva compass being put to use.

So much for how to prevent yourself from getting lost in the first place. If it does happen, a few simple rules generally apply.

Stop, cool it, and try to work out your location. There's a dangerous temptation, when lost, to push on stubbornly (and even in panic) until completely exhausted as well; resist this. Being lost should not be confused with being defeated or anything of that kind.

A few tricks for working your way out of trouble include the following.

● Backtrack. It's often not very exciting, but if your ski tracks are not snowed in, it's also foolproof.

● Follow a stream. If you are in the mountains, this may mean dropping downhill until you find one (if they're not all buried). Running water almost invariably leads to civilization.

● Check for natural indicators of north and south. Know the differences in your area between vegetation types on north and south facing slopes. Also be aware of differences in the color of tree bark (with some species) that depend on exposure. Be familiar with prevailing winds and signs of their direction; near timberline, for example, trees will lean or grow away from the wind. Though it is often unwise to travel at night, know the stars.

• Do not wait until dark to build an emergency camp or bivouac. Allow yourself plenty of time to get set up and sheltered.

• Don't press on until you, or any member of your party, is played out, or close to it. Getting lost is not dangerous itself; the problem lies in the way you handle the experience. If you've left word with someone of your route (something you should always do), a search party will be dispatched to lead you back home.

THE BIVOUAC

A bivouac is an unplanned overnight camp. Knowing how to hole up and stay warm in an emergency situation takes much of the uncertainty out of the experience, and can change it from an ordeal into an exercise in coolness and mastery. The elements of a successful bivouac are as follows:

• Make camp early, before it's dark (so you can see what you're doing), and before anyone is worn out.

• Make the best shelter you can. If there's time, dig a snow cave; if not, improvise the best you can to get yourself out of the elements. You're better off in the woods than out in the open; likewise on the lee side of a ridge, rather than to the windward. You want to be sure to be as much out of the wind as possible. In some cases, you can dig down into the snow and pile up a windbreak. Skis, pole, and pine boughs also make serviceable lean-to's.

• Build a good warming fire; it does not have to be large, as long as its heat is steady and concentrated. Be sure someone stays up to keep it going (best do this in shifts);

it's OK for the others to try to doze as long as they are not chilled. Make sure no one rolls or slides into the fire; burned clothing is obviously useless. In addition, fire can often be helpful as a signal.

• Share food sensibly. Remember—food generates body heat in addition to easing hunger.

• If you are in a situation in which you can neither dig a shelter, nor build a fire, get in the most protected place you can find, and be ready to *stand up* the whole night; sitting down in the snow is an absolute No under these circumstances. Stamp your legs and keep the others in the group moving likewise to keep up their body heat. This is an occasion that demands able, spirited leadership; cheerful people usually take care of themselves better.

WINTER HYGIENE

Much of what might be said under this inclusive heading is scattered appropriately throughout the book. That goes for commonsense measures in preventing and dealing with sunburn, frostbite, and a number of similar infirmities that can crop up out in the snow.

A couple of words do need to be said here about clothing. On a long trip, especially, bring extra changes of anything that's next to your skin. In addition to being dry and warm, clean clothing is also less apt to cause chafing, rubbing, rashes or blisters. Note that two pairs of socks are an acceptable minimum. In addition to being another example of the layer principle, the outer sock will rub against the inner one, which means that much less rubbing against you—which reduces the possibility of blisters. Especially in mid-winter, some people actually prefer three pairs of socks—in this case, primarily for warmth. Always break in new boots on shorter tours before heading out on longer trips; if you're going to have blisters, it's better to have them close to home. A little talcum powder often helps, too.

Regarding clothing in general, be sure the fit is right. Tight clothing can cut circulation and lead more quickly to frostbite in cold temperatures; overly loose clothing generally doesn't insulate as well, gets in the way, and may cause chafing.

HYPOTHERMIA

This is very serious business. Hypothermia is the medical term for the lowering of the temperature of one's inner body core. If that temperature drops as low as 78 degrees, you have a fatality on your hands; since this may happen very quickly (sometimes within no more than a half hour), an awareness of warning signs is imperative.

Ironically, most hypothermia cases occur at temperatures normally considered warm: between 30 and 50 degrees. Below that, people tend to be forewarned and appropriately cautious. The normal progress of a hypothermia case is regular and predictable. The usual prerequisites are tiredness, cold, and sometimes hunger (remember, food is fuel for heat production). Perhaps the person has been skiing hard all day and has worked up a slight sweat, which in the late afternoon turns into a chill. Being wet is always dangerous; water at 50 degrees is much, much colder than dry air at the same temperature. Shivering normally sets in at this point; it is the body's natural, involuntary reaction to chill—its way of trying to generate heat by rapid movement. Hypothermia has not yet set in, but *this is the time to stop and warm up.* Shivering should be obvious, both to the person who is doing it and to those who are with him; it should be taken as an unmistakable warning. Warm drink, high calorie foods, fire, dry clothing, and protection from the wind are all remedies at this point.

Suppose these warnings are missed or ignored? As the body continues to lose heat faster than it's produced, the normal reaction is for the body to cut off the flow of warmth to the extremities—head, arms, hands, legs, feet—in order to conserve it for the trunk and the vital organs there. Early on, the victim may just feel woozy and become mildly ill-tempered in

WIND CHILL

Wind is an element to be carefully reckoned with on any winter tour. If the air is moving at all, the chill factor (a measure of the rate at which heat is lost from the human body) will always be lower than the thermometer reading. This compact chart shows graphically how even a mild 10 mile-an-hour breeze can reduce the effective temperature 20 and even 30 degrees. It was compiled originally by Antarctic explorers but is now used widely by tour skiers and others who venture outdoors in the winter.

WHAT THE THERMOMETER ACTUALLY READS

Wind Speed (MPH)	50	40	30	20	10	0	−10	−20	−30	−40	−50	−60
	WHAT IT EQUALS IN ITS EFFECT ON EXPOSED FLESH											
CALM	50	40	30	20	10	0	−10	−20	−30	−40	−50	−60
5	48	37	28	16	6	−5	−15	−26	−36	−47	−57	−68
10	40	28	16	4	−9	−21	−33	−46	−58	−70	−83	−95
15	36	22	9	−5	−18	−36	−45	−58	−72	−85	−99	−102
20	32	18	4	−10	−25	−39	−53	−67	−82	−96	−110	−124
25	30	16	0	−15	−29	−44	−59	−74	−83	−104	−113	−133
30	28	13	−2	−18	−33	−48	−63	−79	−94	−109	−125	−140
35	27	11	−4	−20	−35	−49	−64	−82	−98	−113	−129	−145
40	26	10	−6	−21	−37	−53	−69	−85	−102	−116	−132	−148

| LITTLE DANGER IF PROPERLY CLOTHED |←——DANGER OF FREEZING EXPOSED FLESH——→|

☐ DANGER ▨ GREAT DANGER

an effort to keep his mind coherent. Thereafter, various more dramatic symptoms appear. Speech may become slurred, and later there may be memory blanks and complete incoherence. Shivering increases and comes in waves; hands and feet cease to function properly (fumbling and stumbling are common); drowsiness is apt to become overwhelming; the person may sit down in a profound, numbed funk and be unable to rise. At this point, hypothermia has set in; the victim is utterly helpless and his companions must act immediately to save him.

Two steps are imperative. First, anything that contributes to the lowering of the body temperature must be stopped, or at least diminished as much as possible. Seek or make the warmest, most protected shelter possible. Secondly, move immediately to provide heat from an external source. The best approach is to strip the victim and get him into a sleeping bag with another person (two, if a double bag is available) who is warm, and also stripped, so skin to skin heat transfer takes place. Someone else should get a fire going to warm the camp as much as possible. Food and hot drink will help if the person can manage them; the food will serve as heat producing fuel and the drink will warm from the inside out. Don't rush this; consuming anything also requires body energy, and it may be a while before the victim can handle food or drink. Finally: don't resume the tour until you're absolutely sure the victim has recovered; full rewarming can take up to 6 or 8 hours.

FROSTBITE

Unlike hypothermia, frostbite normally occurs at low temperatures; further, it strikes the extremities rather than the inner body core. For this reason, it's not considered a fatal winter affliction, though at its worst, frostbite can lead to amputation.

Usually, frostbite cases experience a predictable sequence of sensations; know these and the worst troubles can be dealt with before they happen. The first symptom is a stinging or prickly feeling, followed by pain, and finally numbness. Visually, the skin is at first extremely flushed, before turning pale, then white.

Though it has been studied in depth, medical experts are still unsure exactly what happens in a frostbite attack. Apparently the first step is the formation of ice crystals between the tissue cells; after a certain point these crystals then begin to enlarge by leaching more water out of the cells. Add to this certain physical changes within those cells, plus blood clotting in the capillaries, and you have the tissue damage known as frostbite. When the tissue temperature drops below about 27 degrees F., that damage is usually permanent.

As it is for burns, the seriousness of frostbite is described in degrees—first degree (or "frostnip") being the least severe. The difference is a matter both of depth and amount of freezing; frostnip occurs before the critical tissue temperature is reached, and affects the skin and the flesh immediately beneath it; deep frostbite sets in afterwards and may penetrate clear to the bone.

Treatment for these two degrees varies considerably, so it is important to be able to determine the nature of the case. Frostnip is white and soft; the affected area should be re-warmed as quickly as possible. Hands can be tucked into one's armpits; feet and toes can best be pressed against a companion's abdomen (and kept out of the wind and cold in the process). Note that you want to get the nipped areas back to normal body temperature and no more; fire and hot water will cause further tissue damage. Also, do not rub or massage for the same reason. There will be a tingling sensation as warming takes place, then a purpling as blood begins again to circulate; blisters may also rise, but no permanent harm will result.

Deep frostbite is another matter. The skin will again be white, but this time almost wood-hard to the touch. Treatment is for trained medical personnel only; warming and thawing on the trail will leave you with a litter case. Surprisingly, a person can ski on deep frostbitten feet for a considerable period, even days if necessary, without further significant damage. It's best to get him out of the woods and to a doctor for professional care.

SNOWBLINDNESS

This can be extremely painful, though it rarely results in per-manent damage. Caused by excessive exposure to ultraviolet rays, the symptoms of snowblindness begin with a simple sensation of irritation in the eyes; dryness follows, and then it seems as if the eyes are full of sand. By this time, the pain will be severe; vision will often be defective, tears common, and likewise with swelling of the eyelids.

Treatment is obvious and direct. First, terminate exposure to the sun either with good glasses (with side shields) or gog-gles, or even a blindfold. Then get the victim home, where he will probably have to spend several uncomfortable days in a dark room before recovering. Do not rub the eyes; it's tempting but ineffective. Ointments may be used for temporary relief.

DEHYDRATION

When you're out in the snow (with frozen water all around you), it's hard to think in terms of dehydration; one normally thinks of that out in the desert. However, skiers do lose a great deal of water in simple breathing (especially in dry air, which is common in the winter), and also by perspiration. When this process advances to dehydration, one experiences a general weakness, deep fatigue, and in some cases, a tendency to faint on his feet. A spin-off of dehydration is constriction of the peripheral blood vessels, which in turn can lead more quickly to frostbite.

One commonly held notion is that people should not drink too much water while on the trail. More often than not, this doesn't hold up well in practice; when you're thirsty, drink. Few people can get by on less than a quart of liquid daily and many need more. Dehydration can be treated fairly quickly by getting the victim to drink, but alcohol is not advised.

SUNBURN

This rates further attention here because it is so often neglected in winter. In addition to the direct rays (especially ultra-violet), there is also a very high measure of reflected light from the snow and ice. Thus, exposure can continue even when one is in the shade, or when clouds obscure the sun.

The best prevention is the gradual approach: ski often, but for relatively short spells, until you've worked up a good, handsome tan. If that's impossible, resort not just to normal sun lotion, but rather to protective creams and salves—"sunscreens" they're most normally called. Apply these liberally, and *before* you head out.

That does it for the major special hazards that winter poses to the tour skier. With a sensible amount of foresight, you should never have to deal with any of these.

II

Odds and Ends for Fun

There are some who might say this chapter is superfluous, like a second layer of frosting on a birthday cake. Well, that may be. Certainly you'll find nothing essential here—nothing to help you ski better, to survive in a storm, or even to select what food you're going to toss in your pack for a tour. There are some additional dimensions to touring, however, above and beyond the sport itself, that provide happy enrichment; if these represent that second layer of frosting, so be it.

WINTER PHOTOGRAPHY

This section is for those who are inclined to use more professional cameras, and not the burgeoning hoard of "instant" cameras, which take the skill (and most of the challenge) out of photography in the name of convenience. Because of the extreme brightness of winter light and snow, shooting at this time of the year requires some carefully calculated settings that most of the "automatic" cameras are incapable of making themselves (no matter what the advertisements may claim). If you still prefer Instamatics, and similar products, skip this section.

Snow photography can be especially rewarding if you take advantage of the innate qualities of the winter landscape. The sun is low in the sky and casts long, interesting shadows even close to midday. The brilliant contrast between glistening snow and dark rocks, trees, or shadows is fascinating to play with. Many people who don't do much at all with black and white film during the green leaf times of the year go wild with it in the winter. The snow itself can assume many interesting shapes and patterns, especially when it is carved and sculptured by the wind. There are the fairyland workings of the various kinds of frost. Of course, the touring ski lends a wonderful dimension of mobility to anyone's wintertime photographic endeavor.

The following run-down deals only with some of the technical, logistical matters of winter photography; the creative element is up to you.

Camera

The only realistic camera for anyone to cart around regularly on skis is a 35mm unit; a single lens reflex model is the most versatile type, and is appropriately light in weight.

Film

Because of the abundance of light, you do not want fast film. For color, Kodachrome 25 is a superior, fine grained, well-balanced film in its own right (people using Ektachromes for snow scenes tend to come up with unnatural blues); it is also slow (ASA 25), which makes it doubly serviceable in winter. Kodak's Plus-X, with an ASA of 125, is as good as any of the black and white films.

Exposure

The extremes of light intensity can be a nuisance to the snow

photographer. It's nothing for your light meter reading to vary three and four f-stops from direct sun to shadow; no film available handles such a range truly well. If you expose for the bright areas, the darker will tend to go black and vice-versa. The best solution is to shoot at the meter reading you get off the brightest area, maybe going a half f-stop under. That way, the shaded portions of your work will go on the dark side, but even so this is far more preferable than having the whites thin or washed out. Shooting into the sun can produce a dramatic "starburst" effect (see frontispiece); to do this, simply meter off the sun and let the rest of the photo go dark like it is on a moonlit night. This is but one good example of using the extremes of light intensity, rather than fighting them. Do note, however, that these extremes are normally less severe early in the morning and late in the afternoon.

Dealing with Cold

Cold usually doesn't cause many problems to the snow photographer until after the temperature gets down close to zero. At that point, you will want to take some special precautions. All films tend to become brittle and more prone to snap in cold weather; load with care, and do not advance the film in the camera with hard jerks on the lever. Equally galling is the fact that light meter batteries often lose their zap in the cold; unless you use a selenium cell meter (which is unaffected by low temperatures), you must keep your meter warm—under a zipped up coat or in a warm pocket by day, and in the sleeping bag with you by night. If you are doing a substantial amount of cold winter shooting, you may want to have your camera itself winterized; this is about like what's done to a car; the normal lubricants are replaced with lighter, thinner ones. This cuts down on sticking (or actually freezing) shutters, etc.

If you've been out shooting on a cold day, do not rush your camera gear back into the warm living room when you are through. Condensation will result, messing up your film, having the same effect on the camera as throwing it into a river.

People who wear eyeglasses know this phenomenon all too well. If the equipment cannot be warmed slowly, then seal it in a plastic bag and let the condensation form on that. If you're driving back from a tour in your car, this is not usually a problem, as the camera gear warms gradually in the interior of the vehicle.

Dealing with Moisture

Snow is wet, and it can sometimes play havoc with the photographer. One thing you don't want to do, for example, is attempt to blow fresh snow off a lens; your breath is warm and will melt it. Breathing inadvertently on viewing aperture will fog it too. Carry some lens tissue or a little blow brush to handle these situations. If you're shooting during a storm (this can make for some very effective work), it's often wise to have the camera in a plastic sack with a hole cut in it for the lens; a lens hood will help keep the snow off the lens itself.

Cold Hands

Cameras are not designed to be operated by gloved hands, and mittens are impossible. If it's not brutally cold, use a pair of gloves that can be pulled off and put on easily; when you're actually shooting you can slide the gloves over the top of a ski pole for safe keeping (usually, there are enough things in your pockets already). For colder conditions, some people use those skin tight aluminum foil-like glove liners; these don't get in the way at all.

Where to Carry It

If you're not carrying much gear, accessible, warm pockets are the best place to carry your camera. If you've more equipment, the top of your rucksack, or sidepockets on your pack, are the best alternatives, again because of accessibility; this is less convenient because you'll have to hunch out of whatever is on your back every time you take a picture.

THE NATURAL WORLD

For the summertime backpacker, the natural world is an obvious and immediate source of interest. Everything alive, from small splotches of lichen on up to the largest of trees, is actively growing, which of course is not the case in the winter. In winter all plant life is dormant, many of the birds have migrated south, and a fair number of the mammals have hibernated. The diversity and richness of nature is therefore a little less obvious; nevertheless, it's still very much there.

If there's a particular bonus in the winter, it's with the animals. Those that stick around and stay active in the winter are forever leaving telltale tracks in the snow. It's unavoidable; whereas in the summer, one must search out a muddy or similarly soft area for signs of the comings and goings of a deer, a fox, a bobcat, a hare, or a mouse, in the winter the snow will inevitably record entire travel routes step by step. It will also record those seldom seen moments of life and death: a rabbit track zig-zagging across the snow, stopping, terminating between the wing-beat marks of an eagle or large hawk; the convergence of a coyote and a ptarmigan above timberline in the

And sometimes you'll even see the wildlife itself; these ptarmigan sat still high in the Colorado Rockies.

Rockies, the brief signs of struggle, the continuation of the coyote's track.

There are a fair number of animal track identification books on the market that will open up this dimension of the world of winter. Most are simple identification-type hand-books that leave the interpretation of the life behind the tracks up to the individual. The standby is Olaus J. Murie's *A Field Guide to Animal Tracks*, one of that fine, widely circulated series published by Houghton Mifflin. A few general points will help even the most inexperienced skier-observer in his initial explorations of the world of animal tracks.

The ideal time for tracking is first thing in the morning after a light snowfall (1 to 3 inches) that has stopped at about dawn. This way one gets the best of both the nocturnal and the diurnal worlds. The creatures of the night will usually hole up, or lie low, during the storm itself, and move out when it's stopped; the daylight animals will also start about their normal courses of activity. This doesn't happen very often, but when it does, be ready for a real eye-opener.

After a heavier snow, there will also be fresh tracks, but frequently they'll be obscured by the excess falling back into, and over, the actual prints. In cases like these, you may often be able to identify the animal by the length of its stride. Another trick of identification, when prints are obscured, is to follow the course of the track; if it weaves under low bushes and branches, you can be sure it's not a larger animal, such as a deer (which would have to walk around such obstacles). Some especially low-slung animals, such as the badger, porcupine, and rac-coon, will leave what amounts to a belly track as they wallow through the snow. Mice will leave tail tracks: little footprints with a line running through them.

After the snow has settled in the sun for a day or two, tracks can take on deceiving size as their finer edges melt away. Wind can do this too. Many is the person who is convinced he's seen wolf tracks, for example, when they are only those of a dog or coyote. Be sure to allow for this deceptiveness.

CITIZENS' RACES

The popularity of citizens', open, or all-comers touring races has, in recent years, become almost stunning. Many are the people who will insist they aren't interested in racing and then turn right around and enter these events. The basic principle is to give everyone something reasonable to compete against (after all, this is a profoundly competitive nation)—and that reasonableness is one element that has made these events so marvelously popular, even for the entire family. One family member may go out and simply be proud to cover the distance; the children will more likely be race-oriented and be glad to make it across the finish line; another person will plunge into a race with himself, as a means of drawing a bead on precisely where his conditioning is (or is not).

More precisely, each citizens' race is generally broken down into a number of categories; for example, the events sanctioned and conducted by the Rocky Mountain Division of the United States Ski Association have eleven categories des-

They're off and running. The mass start of the Keystone Kaper citizens' race in Colorado, February 1974.

ignated according to age (at the head of the list is "56 & older;" at the bottom is "9 & younger") — these in addition to three more groups for "licensed competitors." In short, there's something for everyone from the Olympic racer to grandmother.

The spirit of these events is another drawing card; they are, depending on the entrant, whimsical, convivial, or serious. The following broadside for the Nordic Holiday Races, held early each March in California's Yosemite National Park, is typical.

> The first year, participants ranged from second-*day* beginners to established pros. The idea was to set your own pace and have fun—and we did! Everyone did—and 69 of the 70 finished the seven-mile course.
>
> Then last year, registration leaped to 322, and the swishing of skis on the granular snow at the start was awesome. Again, there were kids and grandparents, beginners and pros—some driving hard for a win and some cruising along to enjoy the scenery. Some even paused for a half hour at the breathtaking Dewey Point, to help the soup-station crew pass out refreshment to the racers. And again, it was a tremendous amount of fun, both at the race and at the party afterward. The fun relays on Sunday, very relaxed and informal, drew 34 three-person teams.
>
> This year we are going to have to limit registration to 350 starters. Either that or we'll have to eliminate the party on Saturday night, because there's no place to hold a happy party for 1,000 people!
>
> So get your entry in *early*. You don't have to be a tiger; if you are confident that you can ski seven miles over hilly country at 7,000 feet altitude within five hours, come and do it with us! There are superb views, good skiing, and good people. And lots of prizes for the most unlikely things. The main point is to have fun, see some lovely country, and finish in good shape for the party!

Now who ever heard of limiting the size of a race because of the whoop-de-do blast held afterward? Well, that typifies the spirit of the citizens' race across the United States. A few of the more famous of these are noted below. This is not an exhaustive list; check the USSA office in your region for a full rundown.

• The Washington's Birthday Ski Touring Race, Brattleboro, Vermont. One of the oldest open races in the United States, it dates back to 1963. The course is usually about 15 km. Contact the United States Eastern Amateur Ski Association, 22 High St., Brattleboro, VT 05301.

• Stowe Derby, Stowe, Vermont. This one has been going since 1965; competitors may race over either the 2½- or 7-mile course; usually run in February. Contact Stowe Derby Race Committee, c/o Stowe School, Stowe, VT 05672.

• Madonna Vasa, Madonna Ski Area, Jeffersonville, Vermont. This 24 km. race is scheduled to coincide with the granddaddy of all open races, the great Swedish Vasaloppet. It is always the first Sunday in March, over a tough up-and-down course that beginners are advised to check out before entering. Contact Madonna Ski Area, Jeffersonville, VT 05464.

• Paul Revere Cup, Ft. Devens, Massachusetts. This February 15 km. race has been going since 1973 only, but there were 300 entrants that first time—all of them charging off simultaneously in one of those marvelous mass (or *geschmossel*) starts. Contact American Nordic Skiing Association, Concord, MA 01742.

• Great Race, West Simsbury, Connecticut. Another mass start event, only 5 km. long, refreshments served. Contact Great World, Inc., 250 Farms Village Road, West Simsbury, CT 06092.

• V-J-C Ski Tour, Minneapolis, Minnesota. This large, open race is held outside Minneapolis where it winds through the suburbs of Victoria, Jonathan and Chaska (hence V-J-C). It is a late February event. Contact North Star Ski Touring Club, 4231 Oakdale Avenue, Minneapolis, MN 55416.

• American Birkebeiner, Telemark Ski Area, Cable, Wisconsin. This 50-kilometer event is now the longest open race in mid-America; it is held annually in late February. This event commemorates the great Norwegian Birkebeiner race, which honors the historic rescue of young Prince Hakon Hakonssen by men with birch bark leggings (the literal translation of birkebeiner) way back in 1206. Contact Telemark Ski Area, Cable, WI 54821.

• The Frisco Gold Rush Classic, Frisco, Colorado. An immensely successful family race, 12 km. long, held in late February. Contact Chamber of Commerce, Frisco, CO 80433.

• The Keystone Kaper, Keystone Ski Area, Dillon, Colorado. Another good high country run in the scenic valley below one of Colorado's major new alpine areas. An early February event. Contact Keystone International, Dillon, CO 80435.

• The Butch Cassidy Bank Run, Telluride, Colorado. The famous bandit pulled his first job here back in 1888; the 5.5 mile course doesn't follow his historic escape route, but it's a beautiful run over rolling mountain meadows. A late January event. Contact Nordic Director, Telluride Ski Club, Box 307, Telluride, CO 81435.

Some people enter a citizens' race to dawdle along and enjoy scenes like this one in Yosemite National Park, California.

• The Rabbit Ears Race, Steamboat Springs, Colorado. This course is one of the longest in the United States (40 kilometers), again through scenic mountain country. It takes place on the last Sunday in April. Contact Steamboat Springs Winter Sports Club, Box 285, Steamboat Springs, CO 80477.

• The John Craig Memorial, Blue River, Oregon. John Craig was a pioneer mailman of the early Pacific northwest and this race commemorates his heroic route through the Cascade Range; each modern entrant actually carries a letter which is specially hand postmarked at the finish line. The race covers about 18 miles and is held in early April. Contact Bend Chapter, Oregon Nordic Club, Bend, OR 97401.

• Nordic Holiday Races, Yosemite National Park, California. Two days of races organized around a bash at the Park Service Visitors' Center in Yosemite Village. Contact Yosemite Mountaineering, Yosemite National Park, CA 95389.

• Glacier Stampede, between Anchorage and Fairbanks, Alaska. This race takes place on the Cantwell Glacier; each skier must pack tent, gear and grub for the overnight stay some eight miles up the river of ice. Usually run in late April. Contact Nordic Club of Fairbanks, Fairbanks, Alaska 99701.

NIGHT TOURING

This book began with a good morning, and ends with a good night. There is nothing to quite match a good moonlight tour—the fuller the moon, the better. You don't have to cover any great distance; it's best to stay on a well-packed trail (or at least in very familiar country, because one's bearings can readily become scrambled in the semi-dark. Many will survey the route the day before. Make sure you're ready to handle the cold. You may want to ski with one of those miner's headlamps;

they come in very handy when you're weaving through a woods, or stopping for a warming drink.

That's it. Have a good munch on that second layer of frosting, wherever you find it.

Appendices

A Instruction:
Where to Get It

Only two organizations are now certifying touring instructors in the United States, and both are working together more and more. Contact either one for the source of certified instruction nearest you.

United States Ski Association, National Headquarters
1726 Champa Street
Denver, CO 80202

The USSA has nine regional divisions throughout the United States. For a listing of these, see Appendix C.

Professional Ski Instructors of America, National Office
1801 York Street
Denver, CO 80206

PSIA also has four regional offices throughout the United States as follows:

Eastern Professional Ski Instructors Association
P.O. Box 67
Lexington, MA 02173

Rocky Mountain Ski Instructors Association
P.O. Box 4
Steamboat Springs, CO 80477

Far West Ski Instructors Association
P.O. Box 24
Yosemite National Park, CA 95389

Pacific Northwest Ski Instructors Association
11204 Des Moines Way South
Seattle, WA 98168

In Canada, contact the following:

Canadian Amateur Ski Association
P.O. Box 2566
Station D
Ottawa, Ontario
CANADA

B Touring: Where to Do It

As has been noted already, you can tour just about anywhere the ground is covered with at least 4 to 6 inches of snow. Even the established areas featuring packed and marked trails are increasing at such a rate, that a full listing would go on for hundreds of pages. The spots listed below all have excellent touring facilities. In addition, most offer full instructional programs, and thus are ideal places for the beginner to get a full introduction to the world of ski touring.

East

North American Nordic. This is a chain of seven complete ski touring centers located in Vermont, New Hampshire, Massachusetts, and New York. Each includes equipment sales and rentals, certified instructors and guides, marked and groomed trails, guided group and picnic tours, and, in the words of the N.A.N. brochure, "miles of untracked wilderness." Lodging is available at, or near, all the centers, which are located at Stowe, Killington, Manchester Center and Mt. Snow in Vermont;

181

Franconia, N.H.; Williamstown and Holyoke, Mass.; and Keene, N.Y. Home base for this mini-touring empire is its Stowe Center, Box 1308, Stowe, VT 05672; phone: 802/253-4592.

Jackson Ski Touring Foundation. This sleepy little New Hampshire village goes all out for touring in the winter months, with all facilities united under the aegis of the foundation. Local inns, ski shops and schools, and 118 miles of touring trails form the core of the program. The foundation is active in education, ecology, and winter camping as well; they even take the local grammar school children out twice a week. That gives you an idea of the quality of this operation. For information, contact Jackson Ski Touring Foundation, Jackson, NH 03846; phone: 603/383-9355.

Waterville Valley. This is a complete alpine ski area that keeps up a substantial touring operation as well. Equipment sales and rental, certified instruction, guided tours, and 35 miles of trails make up the touring scene here. For information, contact Waterville Valley Associates, Waterville Valley, NH 03223; phone: 603/236-8371.

Trapp Family Lodge. This outstanding nordic center is run by the youngest son of the real Baroness Maria Von Trapp, the same one immortalized in *The Sound of Music.* Johannes Von Trapp now has one of the top touring centers in the United States, warmed by an ample seasoning of old world charm, with hallways and window sills adorned with flowers from the family greenhouse. The touring program is superb: 60 miles of trails, a battery of fulltime instructors, and a complete shop. There's an overnight cabin three miles out on the trail network. Contact Trapp Family Lodge, Stowe, VT 05672; phone: 802/253-7545.

Adirondack Loj. The cradle of organized touring in the United States, the sport was active here even back around 1900. The Loj provides rentals, sales and instruction, and a 100-mile-plus network, which reaches out into the hills and mountains nearby. The Adirondack Mountain Club, based in Lake

Placid like the Loj, conducts a midwinter snow camping and mountaineering school. Contact Adirondack Loj, Box 87, Lake Placid, NY 12946; phone: 518/523-3441.

Midwest

Telemark. Another alpine area with an outstanding touring program. The trail complex consists of eight well-marked routes ranging from 1 to 9 miles in length; all are designed and laid out by Sven Wiik. The sales, rental, and instruction (both group and private) programs are all complete. Contact Telemark, Cable, WI 54821; phone: 715/798-3811.

Whitecap Mountains. Located along the unique south Superior shoreline of northern Wisconsin (the closest thing to wilderness in the Midwest), this alpine area has a solid touring program as well. The trail system here, also laid out by Sven Wiik, covers 20 kilometers and forms six loops—each one named after a Norse god (Odin, Frejya, Balder, Thor, Loki, and Valkyries). Full sales, rental and instruction programs. Contact Whitecap Mountains, Montreal, WI 54536; phone: 715/561-2227.

Equinox Ski Touring Club. This is the hotbed of touring in the Twin Cities area. Join the club and you gain access to its 30 miles of trails (almost all groomed), plus touring equipment, rental shop, and instruction. Night touring (by torchlight on occasion) is a popular activity here. Contact Equinox Ski Club, 5005 France Avenue South, Minneapolis, MN 55410; phone: 612/929-5573.

The Rockies

Vail. This giant alpine area has its own touring program under the leadership of Steve Rieschl, a former United States national Nordic competitor. Touring opportunities here are vast—everything from the Vail Golf Course to the nearby Eagles Nest Wilderness Area. Contact Steve Rieschl's Ski Touring School, Golden Peak, Vail, CO 81657; phone: 303/

476-3116, or write directly to Rieschl at Box G, Avon, CO 81657.

Scandinavian Lodge. This is Sven's own operation, and *the* educational center for touring in the Rockies. It's located in the heart of LTV's rapidly growing Steamboat alpine area. There's a complete ski touring and rental shop here; guided tours and instruction are available daily either from Wiik himself, or his staff of instructors. Touring trails include a 1-kilometer technique track at the lodge. Longer guided tours in the nearby Routt National Forest are common; this is lovely, rolling mountain country, ideal for all ability groups. Contact the Scandinavian Lodge, Box 5040, Steamboat Village, CO 80499; phone: 303/879-0517.

Ashcroft. This is a genuine, old-time ghost town that harks back to the mining days in Colorado. Located a stone's throw up the Castle Creek Valley from the alpine skiing mecca of Aspen, this is a complete touring area with 20 miles of marked trails (also designed and laid out by Sven Wiik), guided day and overnight tours (there are several cabins higher in the mountains), full equipment sales and rentals, and certified instruction. An interesting sidelight here is Stuart Mace's Toklat Lodge, which is the site of the outstanding sled dog operation in the United States; if you want to take a break from your touring, you can hitch a ride on one of the sleds behind a sleek team of huskies and malamutes. Contact Ashcroft Ski Touring Unlimited, Box 1572, Aspen, CO 81611; phone: 303/925-1971.

Ouray. Consider this one of the fine sleepers in the Rockies for those with a yen to tour in the midst of absolutely breathtaking mountain scenery. Ouray is an old-time Colorado mining camp that has been reborn as a resort in the heart of this "Switzerland of America," as the San Juan Range here is affectionately known. Touring here is conducted by Box Canyon Ski Tours; certified instruction is available, as are a marvelous array of guided tours. Proprietor Kurt Kircher (a veteran of the Swedish army) also runs classes in winter camping, survival techniques, and avalanche awareness and rescue. Contact Box

Canyon Ski Tours, P.O. Box 632, Ouray, CO 81427; phone: 303/325-4551.

Jackson Hole. This is the gateway to Grand Teton National Park, and also to several other of the great mountain ranges of northwestern Wyoming, especially the Absarokas and the Wind Rivers. Jackson Hole Mountain Guides runs an extensive instruction and guided tour program, with a strong emphasis on technique—not just touring, but also the skills needed for self-reliance in the mountains in winter. Contact Jackson Hole Mountain Guides, P.O. Box 788, Jackson, WY 83001; phone: 307/733-4979.

Big Sky. This complete, year-round resort includes an active winter touring program run out of the Black Otter Lodge. The 35-mile trail network includes those used for the 1974 National Championship and North American International Races. The sales, rental, and instructional operation is modest, but complete. Contact Big Sky of Montana, P.O. Box 1, Big Sky, MT 59716; phone: 406/995-4611.

Far West

Mt. Bachelor. A major alpine area, with a vigorous touring program in the heart of the country where the John Craig Memorial Race is held. An ample trail system is complemented by a full sales, rental and instruction program. Contact Mt. Bachelor Ski Area, Route 3, Box 450, Bend, Oregon 97701; phone: 503/YP7-3900 (via Bend mobile operator).

Cal-Nordic Ski Touring Institute. The Tamarack Lodge at Mammoth Lakes is headquarters for this thorough ski touring operation, which includes 25 miles of signed trails, touring clinics, an instructors' certification program, guided tours (including overnighters), ski mountaineering, classes in winter camping and survival techniques, plus the usual in sales, rental and instruction. Contact Cal-Nordic Ski Touring Institute, Tamarack Lodge, Mammoth Lakes, CA 93546; phone: 714/934-6955.

Yosemite National Park. Little need be said of the scenic quality of this great national park. Yosemite Mountaineering's touring program ably matches the superlatives of the surrounding landscape. Instruction includes that in regular touring technique, plus race coaching, children's classes (for ages eight to twelve), and an excellent touring survival course. Guided tours of all levels are a mainstay; several overnight huts in the park extend the scope of these journeys. Contact Yosemite Mountaineering, Yosemite Park & Curry Company, Yosemite National Park, CA 95389; phone: 209/376-4611, ext. 244.

● Finally, those United States Geological Survey maps are highly reliable guides for touring off the beaten trail. When ordering, be sure to specify the precise location you wish and, preferably, the name of the map or maps you wish. Contact the USGS office nearest you.

United States Geological Survey
Washington Distribution Section
1200 South Eads Street
Arlington, VA 22202

United States Geological Survey
Distribution Section
Building 41
Denver Federal Center
Denver, CO 80225

For Canadian maps, contact:

Map Distribution Office
Department of Mining and Technical Surveys
615 Booth Street
Ottawa, Ontario
CANADA

C Organizations:
What to Join

Ski touring clubs run the gamut in the United States. New groups are springing up regularly, while the ranks also include some of the oldest, established outing clubs in the country. To list all of these would take pages on end; the following is but a sample listing.

• The United States Ski Association is involved in all dimensions of the sport; joining the USSA will open the door to organized touring activity to varying degrees in various parts of the United States. If the region itself isn't particularly active in touring, personnel in the office there will be able to refer you to groups who are.

Alaska Division — USSA
P.O. Box 4-2126
Anchorage, Alaska 99509

Central Division — USSA
P.O. Box 66014, AMF
O'Hare
Chicago, Illinois 60666

187

United States Eastern Amateur Ski Association
20 Main Street
Littleton, N.H. 03561

Far West Ski Association
812 Howard Street
San Francisco, California 94102

Los Angeles branch:
1313 W. 8th Street
Los Angeles, California 90017

Intermountain Division — USSA
19 East 2nd South
Salt Lake City, Utah 84111

Northern Division — USSA
1111 North 7th
Bozeman, Montana 59715

Pacific Northwest Ski Association
P.O. Box 6228
Seattle, Washington 98188

Rocky Mountain Division — USSA
1463 Larimer Street
Denver, Colorado 80202

Southern Division — USSA
P.O. Box 918
Winston-Salem,
North Carolina 27102

• Mountain and outing clubs are often hotbeds of touring activity. Here are a few of the more prominent ones across the United States.

Appalachian Mountain Club
5 Joy Street
Boston, MA 02108

(Founded in 1876, this is the oldest club of its kind in the

United States. The A.M.C. has eight chapters in New York, Connecticut, Massachusetts, New Hampshire, Maine and Pennsylvania.)

Sierra Club
Mills Tower
Bush Street
San Francisco, CA 94104

(More noted for its conservation activities, many local Sierra Club groups also have active winter outing programs, including regular tours.)

Wasatch Mountain Club
2959 Highland Drive
Salt Lake City, UT 84106

Colorado Mountain Club
1723 East 16th Avenue
Denver, Colorado 80218

Dartmouth Outing Club
Hanover, N.H. 03755

• Rudolph Mattesich's Ski Touring Council has been a magnificent and tireless organizer and promoter of the touring sport (especially in New England) for more than a decade. An annual schedule of the Council's workshops and guided tours may be bought for $2.25. The Council isn't actually a club, but it's a fantastic clearinghouse that will inevitably get you together with others involved in touring.

Ski Touring Council
Troy, VT 05868

D Books and Magazines: What to Read

Reading matter on the touring sport is proliferating at a stupendous rate; unfortunately, some of it is less than reliable. This list covers a few of the truly solid high points. For touring trail and area guides, see Chapter 6; for books on avalanches, see Chapter 9.

- John Caldwell, *The New Cross-Country Ski Book* (Stephen Green Press, Brattleboro, VT, 1973). Now in its fourth edition, this book seems to improve with each revision. It is excellent on advanced and racing technique. Caldwell's style is lucid and quick.
- Lito Tejada-Flores and Allen Steck, *Wilderness Skiing* (Sierra Club, San Francisco, CA, 1972). A handy pocket-sized "totebook" with much useful information for the tour skier and the ski mountaineer. Clearly written and carefully thought out.

Several magazines now devote at least parts of their winter issues to current information on touring.

• *Nordic World* (P.O. Box 366, Mountain View, CA 94040; one year subscription, six issues: $4.00). New in 1973, this publication promises to be the premier touring magazine in the United States. Articles cover all aspects of the sport.

• *Backpacker* (28 West 44th Street, New York, N.Y. 10036; one year subscription, four issues: $7.50). A beautifully done, four-color magazine launched in 1973; early issues haven't done much on touring, but the range and depth of articles is outstanding. Test reports on outdoor equipment (sleeping bags, packs, etc.) are rigorous, uncompromised and certainly of value to the touring community.

• *Colorado Magazine* (7190 West 145th Ave., Denver, CO 80215; one year subscription, six issues: $6.00). A bi-monthly magazine covering the six-state Rocky Mountain corridor with a steady emphasis on outdoor recreation—including regional touring articles and directories in the three winter issues.

Index

1 2 3 4 5 6 7 ← P Y → 9 8 7 6 5 4